WHO GETS THE DRUMSTICK?

ACKNOWLEDGMENT

To my loving husband Frank, whose head and heart were always as close to the book as mine; to Paul Hackett and Bob Specht for their unflagging zeal and co-operation in working with me on the material; to Michael and Rusty for their efforts and sacrifices with the fighting Marines, thus ensuring that Americans will always be at liberty to write a book.

To our loved ones here and departed

I

It was a morning like a thousand others in our Navy life together. My husband Dick joked with me at breakfast. Married eleven years, we were proud of our seven children. He drank his coffee slowly, speculating about our eighth, now well on the way.

"With four boys and three girls, I think it'd be nice to have another little girl to even things up."

"You mean balance things out."

"Exactly. Seriously though, I've got a terrific name for her."

"Don't tell me, let me guess."

"Go ahead."

"Teresa."

He was really surprised. "How'd you know?"

"Because, my dear, this is only the fourth time you've tried to sneak that name into this family."

He smiled. He was blond and fair, very young to have seven children. Life was good. He loved me and the children. He loved flying. He had worked hard to rise in the regular Navy. Our eleven years together had brought us from Key West to Kodiak, Alaska; from Okinawa to the Great Lakes. Now we were settled in a house at Whidbey Island, Washington.

He got up and checked the weather, as he always did. It was a beautiful June morning. There was a mist which would soon burn off. It was good flying weather. Did he want to say something to me then? Was there something I might have said if I had those minutes back? It is hard to know. He hugged me good-bye; I kissed him. In four hours he was dead.

1

He was flying as a bombardier-navigator on an A3D, a heavy-attack, twin-engine jet bomber, when the thirty-five-ton plane crashed into Puget Sound just a few miles from our house.

The chaplain came to tell me. When his car stopped outside I already had a premonition. I held the child inside me as if to shield it from some blow, for somehow I knew that Dick was dead. Yet I opened the door for the chaplain as if this were a well-rehearsed ritual, or as if it were a social call, not an official visit.

There must have been sounds—the children playing in their room, the sound of planes overhead—but I did not hear them. I stood in my own square of silence. The chaplain cleared his throat. I said dully, "This is an official visit, Father?"

"Yes, Helen. It is."

"Is he just hurt?"

"No. He isn't."

"He's really gone then."

"Yes, Helen."

The next few hours seemed to pass as in a dream. People came and went. And then, mercifully, I was alone. Dick was dead and the years of my happiness were dead, too. I found a chair, sat down, and tried to break through the numbness that had come over me. *Dear God,* I thought, *how can I tell the children?*

Everything was gone from me. All the beauty that Dick had brought into my life, all the moments we had shared: watching the sunsets off the Florida Keys, the million-hued reflections of the aurora borealis, the joy of the children playing around him. The better part of my life had crashed into the sea. How could I tell the children?

I tried to settle my mind on something in that room but it was crowded by hard-bought memories of Dick. I thought: Helen North, you're thirty-two; you've been a Navy wife for eleven years. You've lived with this shadow all this time. Now is the moment for which you've been steeled by Dick himself. But not so soon. I didn't expect death to part us so suddenly.

I stood up, wiped away tears, and fought to regain my composure. Colleen, our oldest, came in from the bedroom. "Who was at the door, Mommy?"

She was tall for ten, with a wise, little-mother air oldest girls sometimes develop. She already knew something was wrong. "What is it, Mommy?" Now her green eyes widened. She was a lovely, olive-skinned girl. So young to suffer such a loss. I spoke slowly, enunciating each word carefully. "Colleen, come into the bedroom. I have to talk to the children."

They lined up in front of me: Colleen; then Janette, not quite nine, solemn-eyed and earnest, so devoted to her father; little Jean, will-o'-the-wisp and uncomplaining; Nicky and Tommy, looking to me so much like Dick; and the little ones, too young to grasp what I was about to say. I thought: Dick, I'm not brave at all. You didn't know me. I'm going to break down right in front of the children. You were all wrong, Dick North, when you said if this happened, I'd be able to make it alone with the kids.

I said aloud, "Now we must be very brave, so Daddy will be pleased with us. Daddy's plane crashed. He's gone to heaven with God."

The little ones were not paying attention. Phillip looked intently at a broken toy soldier. The older children did not show any sign of comprehending what I had said. They each wore a solemn mask. I spoke quickly, conscious that my voice was rising a bit. "Now, when we pray, we'll always pray to Daddy, too. Do you understand?" They nodded. "Well, then, let's kneel and pray to Daddy to make us brave."

Before I could begin, Jeannie's bowed head popped up. She was smiling "Daddy's happy, I bet."

"Why do you say that?"

" 'Cause he can see the angels now. Not like in a book but like they're real people."

Janette was fiercely biting her lower lip as we began a simple child's prayer. I watched their bowed heads and felt the new baby's life moving within me. True, I prayed; yet a terrible emotional undertow was dragging me down, so that not even the sight of my praying children gave me comfort; I only felt an agonizingly sharpened sense of loss.

During the funeral services, I felt that Dick was near me —more, that he was trying to comfort me and assure me I would still have his help from the next life. I read the words in my missal: "The souls of the just are in the hand of God, and the torment of the death shall not touch them. . . . For to your faithful, O Lord, life is changed, not taken away, and the abode of this earthly sojourn being dissolved, an eternal dwelling is prepared in heaven."

The comfort of these words sustained me during the days that followed.

3

Unreal summer months passed. I was able to care for the children in a strange, almost automatic way. Navy and civilian friends came and tried to help. The wife of the squadron's commanding officer stayed with me much of the time.

I had been warned I might have a difficult time in having this baby. I made out a will to protect the children.

But the hour came—and I lived.

My heart was moved by the most compassion imaginable for this tiny girl baby. At times, when I held her, I felt there was something for me to learn through her, some wonderful insight into the continuity of life. But what it was escaped me, and my mind veered away from it. I had for so long been tuned to Dick, to having a partner to share my thoughts and reactions with, that I found myself unwilling to think about things in this state of aloneness.

Dick was dead, yet Teresa was born. I lived. The children lived. Outside the hospital window, the sky was the same; day came and night fell; the universe had not dissolved away, and I had to accept this.

I was alone now and must think for myself. No matter how unreal I felt, I must at least act as the person who existed in Dick's mind would have acted. If I could freeze myself into the mold Dick had cast, we would be united forever. Then the memory of our last morning would come, and the question: If he had known he was to die, might he not have told me something more?

Now even that morning was hazy with time. I had to face the necessity of escaping from this memory, and yet accept it. It sounded easy because the challenge was all blurred, a part of the world outside the hospital. Soon it would focus into sharp lines of loss and pain.

Lying in the hospital bed, I felt tears press behind my eyes. I tried to stop them, said to myself that tears are worthless; but they didn't stop. In my mind I heard again the question more than one well-meaning Navy wife had asked when they noted that my husband had not visited me: "Is your husband deployed?" Wanting to avoid the embarrassment that would result, I said yes. Dear God, how I wished his absence meant just this. How often had I complained silently when he had been away at sea for months on end. But at least then I knew he would come home. This time the deployment was for eternity. Tears washed like an early rain over every memory we shared.

A nurse found me crying. Ann was from Boston, one of

the few civilian nurses at the hospital. She had a little-boy face, quick, efficient movements, and a brisk manner.

"No sense crying," she said. "I heard the deal you have. But let me give you a clue. You just have to step back and dive into your misery. And work your way out. You're no neurotic with her first baby having *post-partum* trauma. You're a Navy girl who lost her man."

I said fiercely, "I'm not looking for sympathy."

"Good. Don't expect too much sympathy from people. They just don't have a great capacity for human suffering. Would you like to watch television?"

"No, thank you." Nothing depressed me more than the senseless world of TV. Its superficial dramas and false sentiment had never held strong appeal for me, but when I had tried watching it these past few months, I had found that even the most trite and overplayed emotional scenes seemed to tear at my own emotions. A family situation comedy which under former circumstances would have been faintly entertaining now unnerved me with nostalgia.

"What do you plan to do?" Ann asked.

I hadn't planned anything. I had held a tight rein on myself up to the birth of the baby; I hadn't planned at all beyond that.

"I don't know. I'll just try to keep everything the same for the children."

"My husband was killed in Korea," she said as she went on with her work. "I have three of my own."

"What did you do?"

"At first everyone was sympathetic. After that I became an unsolved problem. Americans want answers. There's no answer to you and your eight kids. If you stay on the base, you'll become a woman on everyone's conscience. You'll remind every wife of what might happen tomorrow. I'd say, forget the Navy. Go to some city and bring up your kids. But relocate in another area."

The idea was strange to me. "I have to keep the house," I said. "I don't want anything to change. I want everything as Dick had it for the children."

"Sure, honey, sure. I've been over this road. You can take the easy way; brood about your husband, read his letters, look at pictures, handle his clothes, and take all the sweet pain that gives. Or you can take the real difficult cure—try not to remember him at all."

I knew the girl was honest. Perhaps she knew from her

5

own experience that someone had to tell me this bitter truth. I didn't answer, just shook my head. If she wanted to shock me out of my depression, she had succeeded. I was now concerned with the future and the best course for the children. What she had recommended was impossible. I couldn't cut Dick from my heart or memory. I knew if I could sustain the vision of his being with God in eternity, I had no need to do this. Strangely, the nurse's advice made me aware of all those trying to help me. I would go home and work with the children. I wouldn't ask sympathy from anyone.

II

When I went home, I turned to more immediate matters—for one, holidays. As far back as I could remember, the holidays had been very special, magical days for me. My mother was a traditionalist, and no matter what pressures were on the family, she did not let the world outside intrude on our holidays, especially Christmas. I had been raised to enjoy the holidays and looked upon them with longing—much as I did when I first read "Snowbound," a poem in which everyone leads an idyllic existence until the world intrudes and brings it to an end. Now I was aware that Christmas was coming and that for the first time in twelve years Dick was not going to be part of it with me. Nevertheless, I wanted this Christmas to be as happy for the children as it could possibly be.

I remembered one neighbor in Seattle who had gone into mourning for a year after her husband's death. Her children were not allowed to go to any parties or movies. The piano in the front parlor was closed. One little red-headed boy told me they could not mention his father's name lest the mother cry. The children moved in a circle of guilt. I smuggled the boy a present at Christmas because their house had no lights or tree or presents for the children.

I didn't want that kind of Christmas for my children. Certainly I wanted them to be aware that this could not be the completely happy holiday they had enjoyed in times past, but

I was sure each one of them would acknowledge Christmas in his own way. For myself, I could try to remember the birth of Christ, but my heart was closer to Holy Week than to the Nativity—to a time of sorrow, rather than one of rejoicing.

I felt relieved that at least the children would be in familiar surroundings for these holidays. I did restrict the amount of television they could watch, however, because I've always felt that television places too much emphasis on Christmas as being a time of toys and gifts rather than as a joyful celebration of the Child Jesus' birthday. I resented and still resent the flashy merchandisers who try to blackmail parents through their children, using traditional Christmas melodies to promote their products.

That year I am sure I was more sensitive to the commercialization of Christmas than ever before, and I knew it. I was afraid, therefore, that I might not be able to keep Christmas for the children as I would have if Dick had been with us. But this problem was solved for me when the big day came. My family each "adopted" one child to give a large gift to. People from the base came, old friends that I should have known would not forget. They all helped make Christmas what it should be for children: a day of wonder, of rewarded good, wishes fulfilled; a day that slightly mirrored God's great gift to all of us on that first Christmas.

Then it was New Year's Eve. The children were asleep. Colleen had asked me to wake her at midnight so she could see the New Year in. I told her it didn't come like dawn or night. But I did go to her now. I softly shook her, and she asked in a warm murmur, "What is it, Mommy?"

"It's the New Year, honey."

"That's nice, Mommy."

She was asleep again. I went through the children's rooms and kissed each of the eight almost as if the kiss were a blessing for the New Year.

Then I sat alone in the living room. Outside, a single blaring automobile horn sounded in the streets. From a house behind ours, I could hear the sounds of a party. I could easily envision the celebrants in funny hats, blasting defiance into the empty night with their inadequate noisemakers. From the radio came the sounds of a hotel party. I could hear a band endlessly playing "Auld Lang Syne" and an announcer's hushed voice buried in a roar of applause.

Loneliness brings a depression all its own. It is not the depression that flows from guilt, as when you are heartsick

7

over some action of your own. Loneliness is a curious refinement of that depression. It is a shattering emptiness. It destroys your courage to face another day. It chips away your strong intention and corrodes your will. Loneliness can even poison the memory of your love. For if the highest, noblest, and best instinct in us is to love, and we have been made one with another being by love, and suddenly torn from him by death, is not the fragmented state even more unendurable than the original loveless state? Is not the loneliness following the death of a loved one more cruelly punishing to you than if you had not loved at all?

If I had been a bigger person, I felt, a woman of deeper faith, I would have used the love I'd had to reach the source of all love, the Divine. Perhaps the despair of loneliness lies somewhere in guilt. Maybe the lonely are subconsciously guilty for not having used this link to the eternal before their loss. I don't know.

Even in my loss, I should have been capable of a universal Christian love of man. For we are all to share Dick's fate. It is every man's fate. Yet the loneliness came often and the New Year stretched before me.

Strangely enough, there were times when I felt a kind of reverse strength. A fierce determination would come over me, and I would resolve that no matter what happened I would raise my children without help from anyone. I would lean on no one—neither friend nor relative.

At other times I saw the life before me as a tiresome procession of years; years of holding hot hands when the children were feverish; of rubbing arms and bringing glasses of water; of hearing lessons; of preparing meals, ironing dresses and young men's shirts. None of these duties did I mind—only the loneliness, the loneliness.

As I sat in my living room alone with these thoughts, my phone rang. It was my sister Kay, calling from San Francisco. It was just like her to remember me now.

"Happy New Year, Helen."

"Thanks. The same to you. How did you know I wouldn't be asleep?"

"I think I know you better than you know yourself. How are the children?"

"Fine. They're all asleep."

"Remember when we used to try to stay awake until midnight? We never made it."

I nodded into the phone.

"And remember the night we decided to sit up on the floor so we wouldn't fall asleep? You kept dropping off. I talked and talked, but you fell asleep anyway. I shook you and talked some more. Finally you said, 'I don't care,' hit that bed, and went sound asleep."

For a moment I was a little girl again. "What happened to you?" I said. "You went to bed, too."

"Of course. There's no fun waiting for the New Year alone."

I thought: No, Kay, there is no fun in waiting for the New Year alone. I asked her, "Are you coming up to visit?"

She said she couldn't, then she said, "Helen, why don't you make this the year you leave Washington? Come down here. The weather is great for the children. You'll feel like a new person. Promise me you will."

I promised Kay I would think about it, and I did, all during the following week. It would be pleasant to be near Kay again. Kay and I had been close in our childhood. She was a joy in our family. Whenever she entered a room, everyone waited for her to tell some joke or describe some outrageous adventure. She had always been able to make my mother and father laugh. This took timing, skill, and intuitive diplomacy, and Kay had them all. I found myself wanting to be close to her now, even if it meant cutting roots even more vital than our life on the island.

I was born in Seattle, where my father was in the lumber business. My mother I always saw as a lady of an earlier era, very formal and aristocratic, clinging to manners which were obsolete. My father was many things to various members of our family. To me, he was slightly withdrawn, bitterly fighting to save a depression-wracked business. To my older brothers and sisters he was a heroic figure, boldly, confidently moving in the lumber business he knew so well. I guess this is as it should be; each child has a personal image of his parents, a mental photo taken at some period of the parents' lives. My mother was a woman with genteel manners and a great sense of fun. I did feel she was too strict at times, but if she was inflexible in many of her ideas she was also unfailing in her love.

I remember Mother's reaction to my first dates with Dick. I had met him in Seattle, where I was working at Providence Hospital. Dick stopped at our house with a friend of the family. He was twenty-three, a tall, blond boy who was already a chief petty officer. Later, he told me he knew immediately we would be married. As we dated and he became serious about me, my mother was alarmed. I was too young, his work was too dangerous, he was not of our faith. She pressed these arguments continually while, unknown to me, Dick was taking instructions to become a Catholic. Every objection to our marriage, real and fancied, gradually melted away as we fell more deeply in love. And by the time Dick and I were married in Seattle, Mother heartily approved of the match. In fact, she may even have felt it was her own idea.

In going to California, I would be leaving the scenes of some of the best memories of my life. And although I knew it would be a good thing for the children, the decision was a hard one to make.

I made it one night a couple of weeks after I'd spoken with Kay. A storm had been forecast, so I'd put the children to bed early. Outside the house the night was black and the wind had been rising steadily. Gradually it became wilder, until the branches of trees began lashing at the windows. Apprehensive, I thought I'd call Kay again. With her good humor and high spirits, she was certainly the one to talk to on such a night.

I started to dial, then stopped as I heard a huge, tearing sound from above. At first I thought a window had blown in, but when I searched through the house I was relieved to find everything was all right. My relief was short-lived, however, for a few minutes later a leak appeared in the living room ceiling. I put a pot under it only to see water dripping from another place. Colleen came in and said there was a leak in her room, too.

Putting on a coat, I got out on the roof. What I saw made my heart sink: the wind had ripped the shingles off and the tar paper was flapping in the gale. Rain was pouring into the house. Fortunately, the ripped section had not blown entirely off the roof.

I ran downstairs to get a hammer and nails. The water was really pouring in now and all the children were awake. I told Colleen and Janette to do the best they could with pots, found the hammer and nails, and went back up to the roof. Retrieving the tar paper, I put it back into place and started driving nails while the wind kept trying to tear it away and the rain soaked me to the skin. Just when I thought I was winning, another part of the roof began to tear. Before I could get to it, it had been ripped off and blown away. Then the part I had nailed down began to flap here and there and I realized I'd have to get help.

In the living room Colleen had Janette, Nicky, and Tommy sitting on the couch. Despite the fact that water was now running down the walls, the children were calm. I think that the next twenty minutes were probably the wildest I have ever gone through.

Colleen asked, "Is the roof fixed?"

"No," I said, going to the phone. I dialed the number of a good friend and tried to calm myself. "Doris," I said, "this is Helen. I've got problems. The roof just blew off our house—"

"Oh, no!" Doris cried. And then she hung up.

I stared at the silent phone, feeling hurt and deserted. Then I became too busy to feel anything. Water began to drip, then pour, from the ceiling light fixture, and for the next fifteen minutes the children and I ran around with mops, pails, rags, everything we could find to stop leaks with. In between we put some clothes in suitcases and packed up whatever we'd need in case we had to leave.

Then the doorbell rang. I went to answer it and there standing on the porch was the friend I'd called, accompanied by three couples—mutual friends—all loaded down with pots, pails, mops, and tools. They all went to work right way, and Doris explained why she had hung up. When I'd told her the roof blew off she was so horrified, she said, that the only thing she could think to do was to start calling everyone as quickly as possible. And she meant *everyone,* for following their entrance more people kept arriving. At one point I didn't know whether to laugh or cry. Fifteen people were moving all over the house, inside and out. Tar paper had been brought and big pots of tar were boiling on the stove. Water was everywhere—on the walls, the furniture, the rugs. Everybody was shouting at everybody else, the ceiling shook with hammer blows and footsteps, while over it all came the moaning of the wind and the roll of thunder.

After a while the storm subsided. Everyone was jubilant, certain it was over for good. The repairs were finished on the roof and we all congratulated ourselves on a job well done. The children were put to sleep in the remaining dry beds and everybody began to leave. The friend I'd called was the last. Standing by the door she said, "Just look at that living room, will you?"

We looked. It was awful. The whole house was a complete

11

ruin. Pots and pans and rags were still all over, catching the last few drops. In the center of the living room was an empty garbage can that someone had brought in when the downpour from the ceiling fixture had filled every other available container.

"I'm sorry, Helen," my friend said. She smiled, and in unison we cried mockingly, "It can't get any worse!"

We were wrong. Less than an hour later the light drizzle that had continued after the storm turned once more into a heavy rain, and the wind began to rise. I knew the house wouldn't hold, and even before the familiar crack of ripping tar paper came, I had all our luggage packed and the children dressed, ready to move to a motel. When we went out the door the garbage pail in the middle of the living room was already overflowing with water.

For the children it was an adventure, and they piled into the car bubbling with excitement. I myself was feeling numb. I was afraid to feel anything for fear I would burst into tears. The rain was lashing itself against the car, making it difficult to see ahead. Unconcerned, the children laughed and sang as we drove along the wind-swept road, as if nothing had happened at all.

I didn't break down until after we'd checked in at the motel and the children were once again in bed. Then, sitting alone in the tiny kitchen, I cried. It was then that I decided to leave Whidbey Island and find a new life for the children and myself.

One day I placed the children with friends and flew south. Kay met me.

"Helen, you look lovely," she said.

I was badly dressed for San Francisco. The months of loneliness had marked me; the northern winter immediately showed me to be a stranger to California. But Kay swept that all aside.

"Helen, I know just the style house you need, a great sprawling house with plenty of room, attics for the children on rainy days. The city is full of them."

I couldn't help smiling. This would be Kay's idea. A rundown mansion might be the ideal home for a growing family, but who could clean such a house or repair it, or fix the plumbing? It was romantic, but I had lived in enough old houses that needed repairs every minute. However, I had no inclination to stop Kay's flowing enthusiasm.

"Remember when we used to play in the attic, Helen? I

was going to be the great lady. Remember my graceful entrances dressed in Grandma's clothes?"

I thought: *How much I remember, Kay.* You made Daddy laugh during the hard times of the depression, when his business was in trouble. The tight, bitter lines would relax when he listened to you. And the things you saw coming home from school, things the rest of us never noticed—they delighted Daddy. Georgie Meadows deciding he could use an umbrella as a parachute and jumping from a second-story window into the snow. And when you described the fall, you mirrored fat Georgie's face all the way to the pavement. Daddy laughed because it was absurd. Especially Georgie's fat, confident dignity. I remember the double dates, Kay, or the times when one boy would visit us both. You would lead him on until neither of us could remain serious. The boy from Quincy, Washington, who tried to impress us with his social position, saying smugly, "Did you know I'm from the first family of Quincy?" You slowly repeated his words, "The first family of Quincy," then added—"Washington?" We couldn't stop laughing and the boy ruefully admitted it never occurred to him what a small town Quincy was.

I remember too how awed you were at Dick's love for me, how kind to the children. I know all these things, but I can't tell them to you. I can just hug you.

So I hugged her and she brought me to her apartment, chattering all the way. She had dinner ready, and my brother Bob joined us. He is a teacher, with a great empathy for children. A mathematician, Bob wanted to know practical details immediately. What type of house did I need; how many bedrooms and baths? I could see that his matter-of-fact outlook chilled Kay's romanticism. I was content to let the wave of their familiar talk comfort me.

Poor Bob took over the job of house-hunting with me. His clear, logical mind was appalled by my reasons for turning down one house after another. He would check structure, plumbing, electrical outlets, as well as all the obvious necessities, then look hopefully at me. I'd shake my head. Driving to the next listing he might remonstrate with me—the house was in a good neighborhood, there were fine schools, a play yard for the children. What more could I want? I'd just answer, "I think I'll know it when I see it."

I couldn't find the house I wanted in Alameda County for a price I could afford. I talked with an architect about the possibility of building. We made an appointment for the next morning. But before I could keep the appointment, a real estate woman called me, telling of a house in San Leandro which had just been listed with her. I drove over to see the house, walked inside, and knew immediately that this was the house for which I had been looking. Later I tried to explain it to Bob. I just knew it was the right house. I forgot to check all the things he had so carefully watched for in our earlier looking. He just shook his head. Kay was delighted.

The house was on a large lot. It had five bedrooms. There probably was not too much to distinguish it from many other houses we had seen. But I felt happy about it. I found I could enroll the children in the local parish school and headed back to bring them down with me. The children were delighted to be together again; and to be a "moving" family once more.

The day of the actual move into the house was a family adventure of the kind we had formerly had so often. And later that night, when Colleen, Janette, and Jean were still awake, they wanted to talk. I made hot chocolate and sat with them.

Colleen asked, "Mommy, are we settled now?"

I was tired from the moving. "We certainly are."

"For always?"

"I hope so."

"You know what Janette is worried about?"

Janette interrupted. "I'll tell her myself." She hesitated.

I said impatiently, "Come, Janette, what is it?"

"You won't marry again, will you? We don't want another daddy."

"Of course not. Where did you ever get such an idea?"

"A girl in Colleen's class—her mother got married again after her father died. She didn't like it at all."

"Well, you three finish your hot chocolate and start thinking about getting clothes ready for the new school."

Colleen asked, "Do you think California schools are ahead of the schools in Washington?"

"Don't worry about that tonight. I don't think they are."

The next morning I drove over to recheck the school arrangements with the local pastor. He had assured me he would have room for the children. I thought I might be able to register them even though it was Sunday. I wanted as little confusion as possible on that first day of school. The pastor remembered me, much to his embarrassment.

"Mrs. North, surely you're not moved in already?"

14

"Yes, Father, we are. Of course we're not entirely settled."

"I have bad news on the school. Sister Superior tells me she hasn't a crack of space. Not even for the tiny ones. It's my fault. I was sure we could fit your youngsters in, somehow."

I was disappointed, but the poor man was so abashed, I tried to put him at his ease. He was a big, friendly Irishman whose heart and imagination had made him promise desk space he couldn't provide. I said, "Maybe next year, Father."

But he did have ingenuity left. "Listen, I'll tell you what. In the next parish, there's a crackerjack of a Mother Superior with a fine school. Actually, I think your new house is just within their parish boundary. Why don't you ride right over to see her now? I'm sure she'll be able to fix you up."

I drove over. I had no idea whether our house actually was in the new parish, St. Leander's, or whether Father, in his bright hope, had mentally readjusted the boundaries to include our new house. Actually, I had very little hope that there would be any more room in this other school.

I had a strong reason for wanting the children in a parochial school. Since Dick's death, I had been unusually close to them, and so was deeply concerned with the hundreds of things I felt they were not aware of. There was no magic way for me to teach the children religion or love, or anything I had learned from my life. I would have to try to teach Dick's ideas of honor, courage, and rightness. When a parent realizes all the learning his children have to do, it appalls him. So it was with me. I wanted so much for the children to be better than I. Yet I knew each one of them must learn each lesson alone. If I tried to tell them too soon what I had learned, their little heads wouldn't understand it or hold it inside. God had so arranged their minds that perception was very gradual. My children had been forced to comprehend the fact that their father had been killed. Even this they sometimes forgot. It was almost as if they expected him to return from some tour of duty. At times the little ones ran into the house expecting to find him. So I was faced with the enormous tasks of waiting patiently while they grew and learned, and trying to prevent them from being too hurt along the way.

All of this was perhaps why I felt so strongly about their school. If Dick were alive, it would not have been so important to me. I felt that in a parochial school the children would find a stricter discipline. This might fill some of the void in discipline Dick's death had created. Being a mother

15

without a husband is difficult. If a religious school assumed some of the burden, I would feel better about everything. That was why I drove so anxiously to St. Leander's convent.

Sister Mary Eleanor, the Superior of the school, was a short, pleasant nun with wise blue eyes that studied me through rimless spectacles. She received me in the parlor of the convent. It was incredibly cleaned and waxed, as all convent parlors are. Sister looked at me carefully as I explained that I had moved into the parish. Somehow I felt she was peering at me in order to judge what type of child I had been, and from that would make a pretty good guess as to the type of adult she was faced with.

She handed me some application papers. "Naturally, we're overcrowded. Let me try to fit your children in. Was your husband transferred to this area?"

I hesitated before I answered. Then I said simply, "No, my husband was killed when his Navy plane crashed."

"I'm sorry. And you have all these children to care for. Don't worry, then. I'll find room for these children if I have to teach them myself."

I was moved by Sister's sympathy. She told me then of her brother, a warrant officer named Frank Beardsley, whose wife had only recently died from undetected diabetes. She had gone suddenly into a coma one Sunday, and died the following morning, leaving him with ten children. I said it was probably worse on a man to be left with all those children.

Sister shook her head. "It's quite a coincidence, my brother and you. Both of you left with large families. I suspect you are taking the loss better than he. Let me help you fill out those forms right now and the little ones can start class tomorrow."

When I reached home I felt very elated. I was deeply pleased to have school settled, and the wonderful feeling of having met a truly competent person with a good heart stayed with me despite my tiredness. That night I felt so grateful to Sister that I wrote her a note thanking her for her kindness. As an afterthought, I enclosed a prayer which had been some comfort to me and asked Sister to forward it to her brother. That afterthought was to change my life and the lives of my children.

III

I worked on the new house furiously. I wanted everything to be as good for the children as I could possibly make it. As I look back now, though, I realize that the rhythm of the house moved far too much in tune with the children. A home has to be large enough to contain two worlds, one of adults and one of children. The adults must not become captives in the children's world. The children must not become prisoners in an adult world they cannot comprehend. The worlds must co-exist in one home with love as the universal language. The children are then not forced out of their sphere before they are ready, yet they know there is an adult life into which they must one day pass. They are exposed to some of that life by the parents they love.

In the new house I had no life away from the children. I was, of course, expurgating some of my loss and grief by burying myself in their lives. But I didn't notice it. When childish quarrels broke out over toys or games, and when tempers grew short in the deadly hours between 4 and 6 P.M., I found the strain almost unbearable.

Kay and Bob both visited often. They must have been aware of what was happening, for they began a simultaneous campaign to have me go out on dates. The idea was foolish to me.

Kay took a breezy note. "Helen, you're really putting out all your energy on the children. But you're an adult. You should have some life of your own. You have to talk with adults. Let's go out on a date together."

The idea was so absurd that I laughed.

Bob, the teacher, was more discreet.

"You do need more adult companionship, Helen. You're centering your whole life around the children. It's not good for you or them."

I think I resented this line of reasoning, maybe because Bob was never easily able to explain his recommendations.

Of course, there was truth in what they both said. There was no adult life for the children to imitate. Nicky and Tommy had become very dependent on me. They followed me around like quiet little shadows. Worse, the older girls, Colleen and Janette, and Jean, just a child, had become very upset when a dear friend of Dick's visited me with his wife. I saw them in the driveway and ran out and spontaneously threw my arms around Tom. That night all three girls were upset. I explained Tom was one of their daddy's closest friends. But they chorused, "You didn't have to hug him."

So when Kay arranged a double date for us with two electronics manufacturers, I went along. I knew that after eleven years of married love, dates would be unreal, some sort of childish pantomime. It might be fun to watch Kay on a date again. But married life changes you. Not only that, life as a Navy wife gives a broader pattern to your thinking, conversation, to the books you read, even your selection of hobbies. I tried to tell something of this to Kay, but she only stared at me.

"Helen, you're free to date now. Dick would never have expected you to become like the widow Schneider."

Kay had pulled a string and out popped a character from the past we shared. The widow Schneider always wore black and never smiled. She made regular trips to church, the cemetery, and the stores. The one trait which frightened people away from her even twenty years after Mr. Schneider's death was her habit of describing his long, final illness with all its horrors (he had died of cirrhosis of the liver).

Kay watched me. "I didn't mean that to be fresh," she went on. "But what was the widow Schneider trying to prove?"

"I just never thought of myself as free to date."

"With eight children, you have to go out, if only to hear some adults talk. I'll watch the children while you do up your hair."

When we met our dates, my first shock was the age of the men. I whispered to Kay, "Aren't we dating much older people than we used to?" She nudged me, and tried to keep from laughing.

"We're much older, too."

Naturally. But time had in some way frozen my memory for dates at a far earlier part of my life.

How can I explain my date? He was from a large corporation and spent a good deal of time abruptly discussing busi-

18

ness. Kay had told him I was a widow but I was very certain she hadn't mentioned the eight children.

We had dinner and danced. He danced like someone who had taken lessons. When we went back to the table, he was saying, "I wouldn't date a divorcée. It's always her husband's fault and they always have to tell the story. There is a crack in divorcées. Single girls are a little too silly for me. Widows combine the maturity and poise I like in a woman."

"What business are you in?" I asked.

"Electronics. The field of the new millionaires. You know how much of the defense dollar is now pouring into electronics?"

"I have no idea."

Mercifully, at this point Kay returned to the table with her date and saved me the statistics. She could see that all was not going well. The men referred to a joke they had read in *Playboy*. It was some minutes before I realized *Playboy* was a magazine. It was almost as if a whole new code had been adopted in the past decade. I felt I should say "Twenty-three skidoo," something from out of the distant past. I nudged Kay under the table. Then I said to the electronics magnate, "I'll bet there's something Kay didn't tell you about me."

Kay shrugged her shoulders and grinned. The man leaned forward expectantly. "I love to hear secrets."

"I'm also a mother."

"That's lovely. Really nice."

"With eight children."

He looked as if he had swallowed a cold fishball. His eyes popped, his gray face flushed. The mere number stunned him.

His friend recovered. "You look so young. How do you manage with all those children?"

"There's safety in numbers."

My friend managed to say, "I think that, too."

As Kay described it later, it was the only date in her life that turned into a PTA meeting.

On another occasion, I found myself in a situation even more unreal to me, sitting in a coffee house with a young man who listened to his own words as he talked. A background of guitar music gave him time to stage sufficiently impressive pauses.

"The whole age depresses me. The bomb and the race to destruction. All this I find utterly depressing."

19

"I think it's an exciting age," I replied. "This is the age in which man begins the exploration of the universe."

He didn't answer me. He acted as if there were some invisible, soundproof glass shield between us. He said, "I believed for a time in Zen."

"Contemplation?"

"But I gave it up."

"Then you're a former contemplative."

My companion looked at me without humor. I wondered if humor had died in the world outside while Dick and I laughed our way through great hardships. He said in the same serious tone, "You might say I'm a former contemplative. I have a new philosophy of total commitment to life."

He slowly drank his coffee. He didn't strike me as having enough energy to be committed to anything. I asked what involvement this meant, exactly. He answered with some animation.

"Total involvement to life means that I, like Douglas Fairbanks on the late shows, am totally committed to life. Involved. Involvement with life and all its forms. That's my new philosophy."

"I'm rather involved in life myself," I said. "Committed to a number of living things." By now I was very homesick for eight of them.

He looked very profound. "Naturally, we must be involved with each other."

"And does this philosophy involve you with children?"

"Children?"

"Yes, I find my commitment to life involves children. Didn't you know? I have eight children."

For only a second the mask dropped. He looked then like a stunned little boy. But he recovered. "I hadn't thought of involvements resulting from commitment. I mean, if you extend commitment to love, then naturally you have a situation on your hands."

"Especially if you're committed to life in all its forms."

"Yes. I haven't sufficiently developed this theory. I could end up with fourteen children as my great grandfather did." He sounded so appalled I couldn't help laughing. The guitar played subdued music and I had completed another assignment as a widow on the town.

Later that night I called Kay. I told her I wanted to be near her and Bob for the children and myself. But no more dates. She agreed. When I put the phone down, I sat listening. The house was still. The girls had finally gone to sleep. I was happy with the house. Here I could bring up the children. It would be a good house. I went into the bedroom and opened a window. For a minute I was held by the silence. Then I knew why. I could no longer hear the sea. It disturbed me, and I closed the window.

IV

On the seventh of March one of Dick's best friends, Commander Russell Moore, was killed at Oak Harbor while landing an A3D. When I heard about it, I felt the deepest sympathy for Martha, Russ's wife. I decided to write her and enclose a copy of the prayer I had sent Frank Beardsley, the brother of Sister Mary Eleanor.

But I couldn't find a copy. It must have fallen from my missal. I decided to write a brief note to Mr. Beardsley and ask for a copy, explaining the circumstances.

I received an air-mail special reply that was friendly and sympathetic. Frank Beardsley wrote that he hoped we could correspond, and that he looked forward to hearing from me. When I replied, he said, would I please send him a picture of myself? He enclosed a copy of the prayer and a photo of himself and his late wife. I was startled to notice how much I resembled her. It was almost as if I had suddenly discovered an unknown twin sister. Our hair, height, build, and coloring were the same. I told myself it was nothing; people often look alike. Frank Beardsley's picture revealed a good-looking man bearing a family resemblance to Sister Mary Eleanor. My mind returned to the resemblance between his wife and myself. Childishly, I covered the husband's picture with my hand and showed the picture to Jean and Tommy. Both thought it was I. On a whimsical impulse, when I returned the photograph to Frank Beardsley and thanked him for his letter, I enclosed a picture of myself as he had requested.

A few days later I received another letter from Frank telling me he was coming to San Francisco and asking me to have dinner with him. I was pleased. I knew that a man in his position would be sensible and I knew too that we shared a life experience. It was easy for me to feel sympathetic toward him, certain that a father left with children was in a worse position than a widowed mother.

Once I decided to accept the invitation, I grew more and more excited about the prospect. I called Kay and asked her to babysit. (I felt some pride that this was one "date" I had arranged myself.)

I am forced to smile at myself every time I recall preparing for that first meeting. I took as much care as if it were the first date of my life, enjoying, as the song says, just "being a girl." I bought a new dress and had to go on a diet to fit it properly. The night Frank was to call I made certain that the children were scrubbed and especially well dressed. I even adjusted the venetian blinds so that I could watch him come up the walk without being seen myself. If Kay noticed all these elaborate stage settings, she made no comment on them.

When the door chime sounded, I was caught completely off guard. I opened the door. We both paused a moment and looked at each other. I think I almost felt a sense of recognition for the charming Irishman who stood there. A man in his middle forties, Frank Beardsley had a sturdy build, a nice smile, a round pleasant face, and grayish, light-brown hair.

I invited him inside, introduced him to Kay. As I introduced him to the children, I looked at them through his eyes and wondered where else you could find such an alert, polite, well-dressed family as this. I felt very proud. Frank was charming to them.

Before we left on our date, he stood for a moment and looked at Dick's picture. He asked me, "How long was he in the Navy?"

"Nineteen years."

He didn't say anything else, but later he told me he was very relieved to learn Dick had been a "mustang" like himself, an enlisted man who had worked his way up to his Navy rank.

When we were out in the car, he said, "Your children are lovely. I actually feel as if I know you, from wondering how you managed all alone."

"I've thought about your situation also. I'm sure mine is easier."

"Why?"

"It's harder for a man to be left with children."

"Strange, when Sister Eleanor told me about you I felt just the opposite."

"Well, we both have our hands full."

"You know, I'm actually glad to be out of the house when the children go to bed. That's the time the loss is hardest. And it was the best time of all before the accident."

"I feel that, too," I replied.

He became quiet for a moment. Then his tone changed. "Why don't I take you to one of my favorite places and we'll have dinner and dance?"

"That's fine with me."

We drove from Oakland over the Bay Bridge. I was suddenly caught by the magic of a golden moment. There was a spell in the sight of San Francisco, the great city which lay before us, in the beauty of the Golden Gate Bridge and the purple-misted hills of the city with the dying sun beyond them.

As we rode, Frank told me something of his background. He had been born in San Francisco into a family of twelve. His father, whom he deeply admired, was a former semi-professional baseball player named Charles Beardsley, a noble, dependable, conscientious man who became an institution at the Hibernia Bank where he worked for fifty-two years.

Frank played high school football and won a football scholarship to the University of San Francisco. He joined the Navy after a year of college. From that point on, the story was familiar to me. He served in all the enlisted grades, from apprentice seaman to chief yeoman, then worked his way up to the highest commissioned warrant officer's rank.

We reached the city. Frank spoke very naturally of his wife Frances, and their life together. "I was a very foolish man. I had no worries, a wonderful wife and family. I remember thinking once: God, you made it too easy for me! I was so happy and grateful that I even prayed that God would test me. After Frances died I couldn't help remembering this. I tried not to be bitter, but it was hard. He took the loveliest gift I had."

I didn't find it strange that Frank talked so seriously to me. We had so much in common we seemed instinctively to understand each other. Then he said, "Let's just enjoy the evening and avoid serious subjects."

I liked his attitude and his sincerity. I said quickly, "O.K.

The first one who mentions a serious subject gets fined. We won't even talk about the children. But before you agree, what are your children like?"

"Typical Navy children—you know, born in different parts of the world."

"I know. My Nick was born on Kodiak and Jean at Uchitomari, Okinawa."

"Greg was born on the *U.S.S. Repose* in Tsingtao, China."

"That's funny. My brother Jim served on the *Repose* in China. He was a hospital corpsman."

"In 1947?"

"In 1947."

We arrived at the restaurant, and as we continued talking we were amazed by the number of times our lives had indirectly touched. The incident on the *Repose* unloosed a whole series of enchanting coincidences. We might easily have met years before in Seattle or on Okinawa or at a half-hundred Navy stations in between.

Strangely, I was very hungry. With Dick, I had always prepared a substantial dinner. Alone, I fed all the children at the same time but never bothered to prepare a meal for myself. I never seemed hungry. Now I ordered a steak.

Frank was delighted by the similarities in our backgrounds. They really were impressive. I was born at Providence Hospital in Seattle, where Frank met his wife, a nurse there. I had trained to be a nurse in the same hospital. Impressive also were the number of close mutual friends we had.

We were both touched by the closeness of our lives. Frank began to tell a story about one of many admirals under whom he had served. "This man was so Navy that after he retired he had a mast erected outside his den. When he wanted privacy he ran up a pennant. As long as the pennant was flying, his wife wasn't allowed to 'come aboard.'"

To me it was funny because for years Dick and I had delighted in the alleged eccentricities of high brass. I enjoyed the meal, the first full, formal dinner I had had in months. We danced to the music of a fine orchestra. I had always loved dancing and Frank was a natural dancer with an athlete's sense of rhythm. A gray-haired, short, portly, rather elegant man was doing the Cha-cha with a woman in her seventies. They must have been regular patrons. The music seemed synchronized to their movements. Frank was delighted with them. So was I. For a while I forgot all the everyday problems of a mother, and relaxed for the first time in nearly a year.

Over an apricot brandy during an intermission, Frank said reflectively, "You know, I've always thought Helen was the most beautiful girl's name. Every time I met a beautiful girl, I would say, 'Your name must be Helen.'"

"Did you ever find one?"

"Not until now."

"Careful, now. You'll be fined if you're serious."

"Actually, I have a very beautiful cousin named Helen. Maybe that's it. You've listened to me talk about San Francisco. Tell me about yourself."

I told him something of my childhood, my nurse's training, and my Navy life with Dick. It was a life Frank had lived himself and understood.

The orchestra was playing once more. The elderly couple were the first ones on the floor. I said, "Frank, they're way ahead of us."

We danced again. Actually, I hadn't danced for many years and I found the old pleasure of good dancing return to me. Although it seemed absurd, I felt almost proud that the old couple and ourselves were the only good dancers on the floor.

Back at the table, Frank asked me seriously, "Have you given any thought to your life from here on out?"

"Yes. I'll hold the family together and bring them up to be good men and women."

"Alone?"

"It just happened that way. I know what I have to do. I'm not interested in anyone taking on the job with me."

"I haven't been able to keep my family together. Two of my littlest ones are being taken care of by a childless couple, close friends of mine. My oldest boys are badly hit by it. All the children are. Every one of them comes to me with one plan or another to get back our babies." He stopped. "There, I brought up a serious note. I guess I pay the fine."

I felt a deep sympathy for these children whom I had never met. Frank had now changed the subject and was telling a funny story about a legendary admiral. We danced and talked until two in the morning.

When we got home, I made coffee for us. Frank took the cup and saucer I handed him, staring at it curiously.

"Something in the coffee?" I asked.

25

"No. It's the china."

"What about it?"

"I have the same set at home, Fran bought it."

Later I said good night to Frank and told him I would be very happy to hear from him again. After he left, Kay heard me come upstairs and woke up, saying sleepily, "Happy Mother's Day." It was funny to have "Mother" coming home at two in the morning. I laughed. Again the sleepy voice. "Have a good time?"

"A very nice time."

The voice was more awake. "A very nice time? What time is it? I waited up until one-thirty. What was he like?"

"He was very nice. I had a very good time."

"Let's have a cup of coffee. I'll have one cigarette and we can talk."

I suppose Kay's surprise that I had had a good time on a date had roused her. I was very tired and mentally counted the hours until Nick, the early riser, would be awake. I would get about three hours' sleep. And the day would be long.

"Kay, I'll tell you in the morning, or rather when we get up. O.K.?"

"Sure. One question—you had a real good time?"

I smiled. "Sure, Kay. I honestly had a real good time."

"Go to bed. I'll get up for breakfast with the children. He must be a very fascinating man to keep you out until two. Well, Happy Mother's Day."

"Thanks, Kay, for everything."

I went to bed and fell off into a relaxed, effortless sleep. When I awoke, it was to the sound of a childish squabble. As usual in recent weeks, I could hear Nick right in the middle of it. I had no time to think of the night before. I called Nick to my room for a private conference. Naturally, with two older sisters, he was pretty aggressive. I looked at this little man so much like Dick and I could barely keep my voice stern.

"Nick, all the trouble in this house lately seems to come from you."

"Not all of it. Colleen starts plenty. And Janette and Jean."

"Nick, wait, please. I don't want to start a contest among you. I just wondered why you are in the middle of so much trouble. Frankly, man to man, tell me what you're thinking."

"It's not man to man. It's man to girl."

"Except, Nick, that I'm both mother and father in this family."

He considered this for a while. "Well, nothing's the trouble. I'm just sort of in trouble."

"Nick, you are four-square in the middle of most of the trouble."

"Maybe."

"Come on, Nick, it's true."

"Well." His face now was very serious, with a square little jaw. "Everyone says Daddy died because the good die young. I don't want to die. So I'm not about to be good."

How could I answer this? Possibly the boy's whole outlook on life could hang on an honest answer now. It was too much to expect one person to be responsible for eight minds and souls.

"Nick, that's only a saying. People say it to show us they know how good your daddy was. But plenty of good people die old."

"Doesn't it mean God gathers the good ones double time?"

"No, I think it means that sometimes God may want someone very good with Him. Maybe people would hurt him. Or life would be too much for him."

"Was life too much for Daddy?"

"Not at all. Your daddy loved life. I think that your daddy made a very special sacrifice. He gave his life for his country just as service men are doing all over the world."

I talked more to him, trying to straighten out the ideas he had gotten into his little head, but soon I noticed that I no longer had his attention. I felt I had talked too much and not answered his question. Perhaps my answers had been too feminine for a growing boy. A few more talks like that and I could lose the boy's confidence entirely.

V

What did I think after that first date? I was surprised that I had enjoyed myself so thoroughly. (It is strange how easy it was to dance again.) But more than this, I was interested in Frank, and not only because of a series of delightful coincidences. It was also because I had the deepest sympathy for his situation. The only time he had let his guard drop that first night was in his mention of his babies being "farmed out" because he felt they needed closer attention. The way he mentioned his sorrow and quickly recovered his poise impressed me. All in all, the date had been a very surprising interlude. I wanted Frank for a friend. I actually felt safe because I believed there could be no emotional involvement between us. I was a widow with eight children. He had ten children of his own. I was protected by the sheer numbers involved.

Then a dozen roses arrived.

Kay had asked me very little about the date. Now her eyebrows rose. I explained airily, "These are for Mother's Day."

"Who sent them—the children?"

You could never get too airy with Kay. I answered indifferently. "No, they're from Frank Beardsley, the man I went out with last night."

"You never did get around to telling me about him."

"There's not much to tell."

"Try hard."

"He's a Navy officer, strong, likable. A good dancer. A lot of fun."

"You build a fine corral. Think you can keep him in it?"

"He's a decent man. It'll be nice to have a friend like that."

"Most women would think so . . . Helen, tell me honestly. Would you ever consider remarrying?"

"No."

"You sound pretty positive."

"I am. I know I could never find that much happiness again."

"I think you'd be unreasonable to expect to."

"And I couldn't settle for less."

Kay was silent.

"Anyhow, I have a twenty-year tour of duty, full time, as mother to these children. When they are all grown, I'll sit in a rocking chair and watch life pass by."

The phone rang. It was Frank. His voice was extremely pleasant. "I had to call you," he said.

"Very nice timing. I just got your lovely roses."

My tone was formal and I knew from the way he paused that it disturbed him. He said quickly, "I wanted to ask you to visit us here at Carmel. Bring some of your children, or all of them."

An alarm bell seemed to go off inside me. I know that my answer came too quickly.

"Thanks for the invitation, but I'm still getting settled and there's so much to do."

"I'll ask another time. It was a wonderful evening, Helen. I sang all the way home."

It occurred to me I had sent Frank on a trip of over a hundred miles, around three in the morning.

"I'm sorry I didn't think of your long drive home. We could have arranged to put you up."

"Don't worry about the drive. I floated back. I'm calling because I can't believe I had such a wonderful time. I've been out on dates but they've never had the magic of this one."

"I had a wonderful time, too, Frank."

"Then for heaven's sake, let's go out again and see if it was a pure accident."

Go slow, an inner voice said to me. "We will, Frank, but let me get settled first."

We then began an exchange of letters in which we were both able to air our feelings and find immediate understanding. Sometimes there were problems with the children that we exchanged advice about, but most of the time we found ourselves writing about the continuing loneliness neither of us could rid ourselves of. Letters gave way to a series of long-distance calls and finally to meetings. The deeper we came to know each other the more there seemed to be to say.

I was confused by my own emotions. Though I felt an ever-deepening need for the warm companionship that Frank offered, I felt guilty about going out with him at all. It was absurd, but the guilt remained. Once when a letter came from him that was filled with meaning for me and seemed to cut deep into my innermost feelings I burned it, thinking: *Leave me alone. Why don't you leave me alone?* I purposely tried to hide my emotions even from myself. I did not want to be in love. It seemed I had spent my life trying to catch up emotionally with someone else. I had felt not yet ready when Dick first told me he loved me. I was always trying to match his love.

The time soon arrived when Frank said he was in love with me. I felt an irrational anger that he should be such a fine and thoroughly enjoyable person. It would have been much easier for me if he were not. I did not want to marry him.

I had never seriously considered the possibility that I might marry again. It was impossible. I had come to rely on my independence. Dick had told me once that if anything ever happened to him, he would not expect false loyalty from me. But it was not only a question of possible misplaced loyalty; my whole background cried out against what was happening. It was almost taken for granted in our family that a widow did not remarry. I had many aunts and cousins who, once widowed, had never remarried. Why had they endured the loneliness? Out of some sense of propriety, of loyalty and fitness. As many of us do, I had often just assumed the opinions of those around me without question; now it seemed each new experience brought me squarely in conflict with these opinions.

As I examined my ideas, I felt I was reaching a crisis in my life. The smallest daily act, such as taking a wash out to the line, suddenly left me very tired, even annoyed. Why had I met Frank? Why could I not have lived in this lovely house and raised my children without any further problems?

Or was this just a dream concept? Could a woman actually raise eight children properly without a father? Did they really need the protection of both male and female parents? Was it possible for a woman living alone to maintain the balance and patience necessary for a family?

I did not want to consider love or a possible marriage, even though I valued Frank's friendship. He had a quality in common with Dick: an inner goodness that was reflected throughout his whole manner. It was not at all a dour holiness. He was great fun and he had a charm that arose from inner decency, which I found spontaneously attractive.

I had always thought no one but Dick possessed this charm. I thought I had a monopoly on exceptional husbands, but now I knew that Frances Beardsley must have thought she had one, too.

At times I wondered what Frank's wife had been like. It was strange to think there had been another woman who was so like me in appearance, taste, background, and experience. We looked enough alike for our youngest children to confuse us. We had the same German-Irish extraction. We both went to school and were married in Seattle, trained as nurses in the same hospital, married Navy men, and had large families. All this was understandable, even if it had taken on for me the quality of mystery of the books of my childhood heroine finding traces of a lost sister who had a special message for her. Imagination can trap us all.

The similarities between Dick and Frank were as real but not all as surface-apparent. There were, of course, obvious similarities. Both were enlisted Navy men who had worked their way to positions of responsibility. They had shared friends, expressed themselves alike, and had lived like experiences. But the closest similarity was in the deepest regions of their hearts. The fact was they were both decent men who could calmly assume a role which required the noblest and best in them to be constantly tested. And they could assume this role without any heroics whatsoever.

Even their attitudes toward most things were very similar. Both disliked haggling of any kind. Both had great perception in religious matters. This meant they could judge events simply, in the light of eternity. Both were men of great personal faith. To a man of faith most of our worries, desires, and fears are somewhat foolish. He does not question the reality of these troubles, as a psychiatrist does not think psychosomatic pain is less hurtful than organically induced pain. He just thinks it's a shame we have to have them.

Faith is a gift of God. The thinking atmosphere of our time is doubt and uncertainty. I think something of this atmosphere divided my thinking. Possibly it even affected my reaction to Dick's death.

Both Dick and Frank made simple judgments based on faith, yet their intellectual curiosity was not thereby diminished. No new knowledge dismayed them because God is all Truth and new knowledge leads only to Him. So Dick was excited by flying and the space age and Frank worked hard at his administrative assignment as personnel officer at the Navy Postgraduate School.

I wanted to be ruthlessly honest with myself. Even the thought made me smile: Helen the Uncertain becoming Helen the Ruthless. Perhaps this habitual uncertainty of mine was the reason other lives always seemed simpler than my own; and why others seemed to move faster emotionally than I.

Frank had no reservations about taking over the responsibility for eight more children. He had considered it carefully. But I was concerned over the prospect of ten more. It was not just the support of the children, the physical caring of them, for in this Frank would have the greater burden, the larger responsibility. The question was, was I capable

31

enough? Could I give each of these children his needed share of a mother's love?

More, I had undergone so much hurt at Dick's death, I didn't want to go through it again. I didn't want to love anyone but my children. It was selfish. But I didn't want to be exposed to hurt again as I had been when Dick died.

For the first time in years the image of Lady, a little black dog I'd had when I was ten, popped into my mind. She followed me wherever I went and I was very proud of her. No one had a dog so loyal. I studied the dog pictures in the library encyclopedia and decided Lady was a Labrador retriever. She was very smart and obeyed all my commands.

One day when I was walking across Bond Street with Lady following, she hesitated. I said, with a little girl's impatience, "Come on, Lady." She obeyed. A man on a motorcycle hit her. She had seen him coming, yet she had followed me. She was dead on the street.

There was no way to console me. I refused all my father's offers of another pet. I had been so scarred by the accident I couldn't bear the thought of loving some pet only to have it die.

Perhaps there was similar self-protection in my attitude toward Frank. I admired him, yet I did not want to encourage his feelings toward me. On the other hand, I was constantly preoccupied with things he said and welcomed his letters and phone calls. He told me he himself was living in an unreal state. His mind was split between his duty—the slow-moving details of his service life—and his growing feeling for me.

At last I agreed to visit Frank's home in Carmel to meet his children, hoping to be disappointed, discouraged enough to slow down the rushing pace of his emotions.

I took Colleen, Janette, Jean, Nick, and Tom with me to Carmel. It was a beautiful drive. Frank had reserved rooms for the children and myself at the Highland Inn, outside of town. The view of the Pacific from the lobby was breathtaking. A huge picture window overlooked the sea and one of the most beautiful coastlines I have ever seen.

Frank lived in a large gray house, set high on a knoll overlooking the hills where the Carmel Basilica is built beside the sea. I was nervous about meeting his children. I was introduced to the three oldest boys—Mike, Rusty, and Greg—and to Rosemary, a lovely twelve-year-old with dark eyes and hair and a charming smile. The others blurred together in my mind. It would take some time to identify names with the younger faces. My girls ran off to look over the house with the younger Beardsley children. I was surprised by the calmness and order in the house. Frank and I sat in the living room and his boys prepared dinner. There were no catastrophic sounds, so I was reassured.

Rusty served us each a perfectly blended cocktail, with admirable poise. As I turned to remark on this to him, I caught him giving his father one of the grandest winks I had ever seen. I pretended not to notice, so I wouldn't embarrass a very nice father and son. Mike had cooked a roast for the dinner. He carved and Rusty and Greg served. The meal was complete, from roast and vegetables to freshly baked pumpkin pie and coffee, served by candlelight. The three boys were clearly anxious that the dinner should go well; that I should be impressed; and mostly, I think, that their father should enjoy himself. They also wanted to convey some message to him that they approved of me. I was almost afraid to look up during the meal, knowing how terribly embarrassed they would have been if, for instance, I had caught Greg with his hands clasped over his head in the prize-fighter's traditional sign of victory.

I was very moved by their warmness and their obvious love for their father. But I had to smile at their earnestness. Later Frank said, "I don't know if you've noticed but you sure made a hit with the children, especially the boys. Behind your back, I've been getting all sorts of nods, smiles, and winks."

The idea of a dad entertaining a woman with the children showing their approval was so human, so natural and funny that I laughed.

"I did catch a couple of signs. Greg was wildly waving his thumb and forefinger and winking at you."

"We also had a 'V for Victory' sign. And two hands over Louise's head. You missed those."

"No thumbs down?"

"No thumbs down."

"That's nice."

"About the short time I've known you: I don't feel it's a short time at all. The constant shuffling of our fates so close to each other is intriguing. Your brother Jim, on the very ship when Greg was born; Frances, a nurse in the hospital in which you trained. We might often have been in the same room years ago. Something more—" He paused.

"What?"

33

"You won't be offended, I hope. When you stepped out of your car, my children were watching. I came to the window when I heard the little ones cry out, 'Mother's dress!'" He paused. "You were wearing a duplicate of Fran's favorite dress."

Looking around the house, I had already noticed other similarities. Frances and I not only had selected the same pattern for our dishes; our taste in furniture—even in colors—was the same. It was bizarre.

Frank changed the subject, as I knew he would. But he changed it in the most unexpected way.

He said seriously, "Helen, I'm a student of the direct approach. I may be the most unlikely man in the world to propose to you, but we could be very happy if we got married."

I didn't want to hurt Frank; but now that he was suggesting we marry, I balked, feeling in that moment almost as if I had spent my whole life asking people to slow down emotionally so that I could catch up with them. Frank went on.

"I don't know how I got up the courage to ask you, but I need you and I love you. I think you need me, too. I probably don't deserve a fine woman like you. Maybe I never deserved Frances either, but the way I see it, we're all whirling through space on this planet and no one of us can make it alone. We might if we stand together."

"Frank, I haven't really thought of marrying again," I said numbly. I asked myself: *Then why all the letters? And the phone calls. Why is it increasingly difficult to be away from him? Is it so hard to admit that you're falling in love with him?*

"Of course the idea is a shock," Frank was saying, "but Helen, we're both too mature to need years of dating. We have the advantage of having lived previous happy marriages. We agree this is the best inducement in the world to remarry. We should be anxious to restore our balance again. I think, too, of the children. We have between us eighteen souls for whom we're responsible. Together, we can do a lot for them."

"Frank, you are letting your heart take over completely. You'd be taking on eight more children to worry about. Eight more mouths to feed and maybe eight more sets of teeth to straighten. You'll almost double your responsibility."

"No, I'll be sharing it with you, which just splits it in half. You're right about my heart leading me. My heart is completely enchanted."

34

"No Irish charm, now. Do you know most people are appalled when they learn I have eight?"

"I stun them, too, when I mention my ten."

"If we married and joined eighteen children in one family, we would be almost illegal. Some people would want us banned."

We both laughed. Then I grew serious again.

"I don't want to seem afraid of life," I said, "but I don't know exactly what to think. Maybe Dick's death was such a shock I'm afraid to commit myself to life again."

"I can understand that. I had my own uncertainties. They led me to talk the idea over with the chaplain."

"What did he say?"

"That I had no sense taking on the responsibility for eight more children. He also thought you were coming down here to slam the door in my face."

The chaplain was almost right. I laughed. "That must have made you mad."

"I didn't think you'd travel all this way to slam a door in my face."

"Frank, you still don't know me well enough to marry me. You hardly know me at all. Suppose your Mike or Rusty or Greg came to you and said he asked a girl to marry him after such short acquaintance, what would your reaction be?"

"You have a point. But, to be honest, I was half in love with you when I heard about you. I knew what you represented, and just from hearing of you I had some love and admiration for you."

"What you're saying is that you were lonely."

"Of course I was. And because of it I went out on dates. None of them made me anxious for a wife." He grinned almost in spite of himself. "Until you. My children noticed the change in me after our first meeting. I must have been terrible before. Actually, the way they seemed to go about their lives despite Frances' death bothered me. Sometimes I had to leave the table when they were eating and talking. After I met you, my attitude changed. The children noticed it. They want to have you for a mother."

We didn't talk again that weekend of the possibility of marrying. But as I left to drive back with five very tired and happy children, Frank said, "You will think about what I asked?"

I promised I would. But as I backed the car up to start down the broad incline before the house, I thought: *Oh, no. It's just too soon, Lord.*

VI

Summer had begun. The children were out of school and the tempo of my house changed. Like all mothers, I felt the increased strain of having the children about all the time.

Frank and I saw each other as often as possible, called frequently, and wrote each other constantly. His letters were priceless to me and always contained something to make me smile: news from the Navy and further thoughts on his Grand Plan, our marriage. The idea was no longer strange to me, but each time I thought I had accepted it, my mind would veer away from it. Yet more and more I found myself wanting to say yes, to admit that I needed him as much as he needed me. Sometimes it almost seemed to me that he could sense when I wanted him to write or call.

I remember one night when I finally had the children in bed and sat at the kitchen table completely exhausted, emotionally drained. I was close to despair, when Frank called. He sensed my mood and spent a long time talking to me. By the time I had hung up, I felt enormously better. Later, I worried about his phone bill, but I never forgot how wonderful it was to hear from him when I needed so much to speak to him.

I tried not to allow the fact that I waited for Frank's letters and calls to affect my relations with the children. But I was torn between my commitment to a children's world most of the time and sudden plunges by phone or letter or visit into an adult world of love and possible marriage.

My mother visited me often. I was reluctant to tell her of any feeling I had for Frank. I hadn't discussed it with Kay or Bob either, but of course no matter how cleverly I kept dissimulating, I soon blundered right into a situation by which they would easily know how I felt.

One Sunday, Mother and Kay were over for dinner. We had just settled down to eat when the phone rang. For once, I hoped it wasn't Frank. I had become dependent on his calls to help me through the last hours of the children's day. But I didn't want to have to explain Frank Beardsley to Mother.

It was Frank. We talked for what seemed to me to be a few minutes and I returned to the table anxious to appear as if the call had been routine. Mother waited with bowed head. I began grace. "I believe in God, the Father Almighty, Creator of heaven and earth—"

I broke off as Kay nudged me under the table. I looked up to see everyone staring at me, then blushed as I realized I had been saying the Credo. I began again. "Bless us O Lord, and these Thy gifts . . ."

Mother had bent her head even closer to her plate. Of course, they both knew the phone conversation had been very important to me or I wouldn't be so rattled. Over dessert Mother asked the question for which I had been waiting.

"Helen, was that a young man you were talking to?"

"Yes, it happens it was."

"Is he interested in you?"

"I think he might be."

"That's nice. Have you told him about the children?"

"Yes, he's met them."

Mercifully, Kay cut. "Mother, don't jump to conclusions. The fact Helen talked on the phone for fifteen minutes while we awaited dinner, or the fact that she said the wrong prayer means nothing. You're not suggesting, old darling, that our Helen is in love?"

The old magic worked. Mother smiled, Kay's gentle irony softened her. "I'm not suggesting anything. Helen, you honestly told him of the children?"

"Of course."

She was puzzled. Mother didn't think there was a woman in the world attractive enough to make a man want to marry her and support eight children. I knew if I told her Frank had ten children of his own, the poor woman would have a stroke. She knew by instinct when you were concealing something from her. And she could hit a sensitive spot from twenty paces.

But strangely, I did want to tell someone how I felt about Frank. Bob was coming to take Mother to a movie, otherwise I might have blurted out the whole story right then and there.

As Mother was leaving with Bob, she said uneasily to me, "Helen, you won't do anything hasty, now, will you?"

Ever since I was little, I couldn't help looking guilty if anyone was accused of anything. If a teacher in grade school began to discuss cheating on examinations, there I would sit with a self-convicting, silly half-smile on my face. I felt the same half-smile now and knew that to Mother I must look as if I were about to do something hasty very soon.

After Mother and Bob left, Kay came right to the point.

"O.K., Helen. I know. There's something in the wind. What is it?"

When I answered I almost felt as if someone else were talking. The words sounded strangely unreal to me as I said, "I'm in love with Frank Beardsley."

"You sound surprised."

"I am."

"Why? Something wrong with him?"

"No. I think he's the greatest person in the world."

"The thing that's always fascinated me about you is the way things catch you unawares. Everyone around you knows perfectly well what's happening, but you are always honestly surprised by what happens to you. Isn't it natural for you to fall in love?"

Now that I'd said it, it seemed perfectly natural. "I guess it is."

My answer was equivocal and I found myself wondering why, for within me, without my seeming to have any control over it, something had begun to ferment.

"Funny," Kay said, "how the human heart never seems to follow the rules we make for it. What kind of man is he, Helen?"

He's the kind of man I want to marry, I thought. And in that moment all the doubts I'd been preoccupied with seemed to dissolve. With growing certainty I realized what I had denied to myself up to then—that by some Divine Providence a wonderful human being had come into my life and I was refusing to accept him. Whatever the reason, guilt, misplaced loyalty, fear of what people might think, I was denying to Frank and myself what neither of us had ever thought to have again and now by some miracle was within our reach: love for another, and parents for our children.

"—something wrong, Helen?" Kay was saying.

"No . . ."

"You look like you're in a daze."

38

I was. Everything inside of me was urging me to call Frank back now, right now, before the feeling passed. Calmly, I heard myself say, "Kay, excuse me for a minute, will you? I just remembered I have to make a call."

"Sure, I'll make some coffee. But don't think you're off the hook," she called after me. "I've got a couple of dozen questions to go yet."

All the way to the phone I wasn't sure whether I wanted to sing or cry, but I knew exactly what I was going to say.

In a movie Frank and I had seen together the hero was always asking the heroine if she was scared. Shaking like a leaf, she'd stutter, "No-n-no." It became a private joke with us. Every time Frank would start to talk about marriage after that and I'd change the subject, he'd say, "Are you scared?" I would hold out an exceptionally steady hand and say, "Yes." So when Frank answered the phone I knew he would know immediately what I meant when after a pause I said, "Frank . . . I'm not scared any more."

He did know, and the two of us spent the next few minutes talking over the wonder of it. We had to keep assuring ourselves that it was true; that indeed we were in love, that we had committed ourselves to each other and that we were going to be married.

When I put the phone down I could barely believe it had happened. Kay was in the kitchen, pouring coffee for us. I tried to keep the corners of my mouth from turning up as I asked her very nonchalantly, "Where were we?"

"I was asking you what Frank was like."

I decided to have some fun. When we were little girls Kay always had a "tell" at dinner. She found the most amazing news in our neighborhood to relate to the family. We had rules for a good tell. It could never be anything upsetting to the parents. It could be thought-provoking like a mystery, and of course the best tells of all were funny stories or those with surprise endings. Now I had a great one for Kay. I answered her question slowly.

"He's very nice. You remember I went out with him the night before Mother's Day? You took care of the children."

"Of course. Mr. Two O'Clock in the Morning. What else have you learned about him?"

"Let's see. I told you he's a career Navy man, so we have a lot of mutual friends."

"He isn't appalled by the idea you have eight children? I'm sometimes a bit appalled myself."

"Children don't faze him a bit."

"Glad to hear that. How old is he?"

"About forty-five. I had no intention of getting involved with anyone again. It just happened."

"Don't keep telling me that. Look, I'm the girl who tried to get you out on dates. What else about him? He's forty-five—how come he's still free?"

"He was married."

"Helen, not divorced—"

"No, no. He's a widower."

Kay lit a cigarette and began to pace the living room rug. "Don't tell me. He's Catholic, Navy, forty-five and his wife died. Because he worked so hard for a rating he married late in life and he has two little children."

"No."

"No to the whole story or just to the number?"

"No to the number."

"Five?"

"More."

"I know, eight. Just to make everything shipshape. You have eight children and he has eight children. You intend to share the load and double the burden, or something."

"Kay, Frank has ten children."

"Ten children?" She stared at me, stunned. "But you have eight. If you married, you'd have eighteen children. Gee, Helen, couldn't you have settled for a widower with maybe seven?"

I enjoyed seeing Kay dismayed. "And I'm going to marry him."

There was dead silence for a moment. But she recovered quickly. "Helen, I think I could stand a drink. Eighteen children! I don't know why I'm surprised. It's exactly what would happen to you."

She soon got over the shock. As I brought in her drink, I could almost see her imagination at work, visualizing the wedding, telling other people. She began to laugh. "Helen, this is great. But you have to be mother to eighteen children. How old are Frank's?"

"Michael, the oldest, is sixteen. Rusty is a year younger—"

"You mean he has teen-agers?"

"Of course."

"But you don't know anything about them."

"We were in our teens not too long ago, Kay."

40

"Of course, Helen. Forgive me these strange, conservative reactions. What about the wedding?"

"We'll have a dignified, quiet wedding."

"You've actually made up your mind?"

It was a question from our shared childhood. If I had finally made up my mind, then it was settled. Until a higher order deposed me.

"Almost. I still worry about the idea of marrying again. There's no real reason to. It's just emotional. I don't worry about the children. And I love Frank."

Kay looked a bit awed. She said, "Helen, I believe you. But one thing, this quiet wedding won't work. I know the magazine and news people. They'll sure want to cover the story of a bride with eight children marrying a groom with ten. You'll have to face that. Where will you marry?"

"At the Carmel Mission. Frank would like his Navy chaplain, Father Geary, to marry us. He knows just about everything there is to know about Frank."

"And about you, too?"

"He knows I have the children, if that's what you mean. In fact, because of them he objected to the idea at first."

"Obvious reasons aside, why?"

"He was concerned about our income, for one thing. When Frank assured him we could manage, Father Geary pointed out that I was still a young woman. He asked Frank if we'd given serious thought to how we could take care of any more children that might arrive."

Kay clapped a hand to her head. "I didn't think of that. Helen, suppose you had eight more. You'd have twenty-six!"

I couldn't help but laugh at her earnestness. But then suddenly I remembered what Frank told me his answer to Father Geary had been. "We've talked about that, Father," he'd said. "We feel that our marriage wouldn't be complete without children of our own." It was a moment that had made me aware of how deeply Frank and I had fallen in love. It was impossible, since we had both been so in love before. Yet it had happened. Love has a power all its own to make the difficult possible.

Kay was pacing again. "Heavens, I'm glad you told me first. I don't know what the family will think . . . How about the children?"

"I haven't told them yet. They like Frank. They enjoy his children. I'll have to face telling them."

41

"When will you break the news to Mother?"

"I'll have Frank meet her first. With his charm, Mother couldn't possibly object. When she saw his picture on the mantel, she said, 'What a lovely Irish face,' so I think she's partially won already."

"Maybe. How do you explain meeting two decent men in your life?"

"I honestly don't know. I guess I'm surprised. You'll be maid of honor, right?"

"Just as it always has been. You know, Helen, you have a lot of courage . . . Eighteen children. Wow!"

VII

We didn't face ordinary wedding plans. Besides the normal preparations, we had to plan a house suitable for twenty. Naturally, we had long discussions about it. I imagine that people with plenty of funds solve such problems quite simply. But our own money, even pooled, was not considerable. We had to measure any changes we made in the structure of Frank's house against the amount of money it might cost per foot. These were ordinary considerations, compared to the wonder of our love, but we couldn't neglect them. Besides the cost of things there were other considerations. A considerable one was the problem of the children's sleeping arrangements.

"Most parents just bunk their children together by age," Frank said. "If there are four, the two oldest and the two youngest share rooms. Things like that. What I've done and what I want to do now is to sleep the older girl who is best with children with the younger girls; or a boy with special talent for handling younger boys with them. For instance, Rusty is very adept at handling younger boys. So he could share a room with Tommy and Gerry."

"It's a good idea."

"And think of all the personalities we have on our hands.

42

There's no sense wasting talent. We have neat housekeepers and some sloppy ones. We won't put two good housekeepers together. We can take our time and work it out."

The laundry and housework that would have to be done constituted another hurdle. "Just for my eight, it's staggering," I told Frank.

"That's a rough problem. We can have Saturday as general housekeeping day. The older boys can do the windows and bathrooms. The older girls can do the ironing."

Most people would have thought our discussions strange, but they were very necessary for us. If we were to manage with eighteen children and do anything near a first-rate job, we would have to have everything organized. Organized, everything should go smoothly. Without planning, this could be one of the most confused houses in history.

Frank brought a good deal of common sense to bear on any problem. He didn't believe in putting any avoidable strain on children, such as bunking girls with clashing personalities together. He had an intuitive knack of recognizing a first-rate idea, either in child psychology, education, or home-building. And he had a good sense of what part of an idea was sound and workable, so that he could pick and choose among ideas and find something useful. His curiosity was enormous. He read magazines always with a half-eye out for information which would be helpful in our situation.

A great deal of thought had to be put in on the redesigning of the house in order to remove as many inconveniences to big-family living as possible. For instance, we had decided to add two more bathrooms. The children were to be assigned to the bathroom closest to their room. This would naturally cut down on confusion in the mornings. Our money was limited, but Frank thought from the practical point of view that the money spent for baths was worth while. He designed two new girls' bedrooms, two baths, a large playroom. There was also a large room for the older children that had a long table like those in public libraries, a magazine rack, bookcases, some comfortable chairs, family encyclopedias, shelves for school supplies.

Frank also insisted that part of the alterations should include a decent room and bath for us upstairs away from the children. He thought parents had to give themselves a break. This was a point on which we disagreed at first. I remember our conversation as he was showing me the plans for the revisions. I was very happy with everything else, but the large adult room with its dressing room and bath bothered me. I told Frank that it seemed way out of line to me.

"I think we're getting too much the best of it."

"I don't think so. Adults and parents have rank; they deserve a decent life."

"But a room this large, a dressing room and a bath?"

"Exactly, and picture windows overlooking Carmel Mission. We deserve and need the room apart. We need the privacy and the composure it brings if we are to be decent parents. I learned this in the Navy, Helen. People in authority have to have composure to handle responsibility. And they can't have it if they live a confused life."

"So we end up building two new baths, two new bedrooms, one master bedroom, and two rooms for the children to use. I hate to think of the money." I proposed that when I sold the house I was now living in the money be used to help pay for the new rooms.

"I wouldn't feel right doing that," Frank said. "Perhaps you should put that money away for the children."

"No, we're all in this together. I wouldn't feel right any other way."

"We'll see."

"Will we be all right, Frank?"

I bit my lip after asking the question. It went to the heart of the insecurity that plagued me, the fear of being responsible for ten more children. I worried now that something might happen to Frank, for if anything did happen to him I would be left with eighteen children to care for.

Frank understood immediately. He put his arms around me. "You're not to worry. We've been through so much already and survived, we'll make it now. It'll be a tight squeeze most months, and maybe we'll fall behind now and then, but we'll make it." His tone became light. "I don't know what we'll do about financing all these birthdays, though. In August alone we'll have three. Mary's, Teresa's, and Mike's."

"October is just as bad," I said. "We'll have Greg's, Tommy's, and Gerald's."

"We'll manage." He grew serious again. "We'll just have to make it for three more years, and then I can retire. I'll have my retirement pay and I can work at another job. Our income will increase then."

"We can do three years standing on our heads," I said. "I'm sorry if I seem scared."

"It's natural. We were depression babies, you and I. Even if we had fewer kids I think we'd be scared. The depression scared everybody, even Navy men. It's strange how different the new generation is. They expect to marry young, raise a family, find a good job. They never experience that feeling of having no prospects, and being afraid even to fall in love. I missed most of this simply by being in the Navy. You were too young to remember."

"I got impressions: my father's business failing, my older brothers and sisters talking, my dad sitting in the living room very discouraged. Little as I was, I knew the fear."

"One night my boys were watching a television documentary on the depression. They kept asking me about it. It showed the bread lines, the bonus marchers, the deserted farms, and migrants on the road. They could hardly believe it happened in America."

"So I guess a little financial worry is allowed," I said.

"Not enough to spoil one minute of our new life together."

"Frank, we're very lucky. God has given us a brand new love."

"It makes the money problems seem very foolish."

"Another thing; it's strange, but exploring the personalities of each of the children is exciting. I find I have a little section of my heart not entirely committed to you in which I love each of them."

Frank was deeply moved. I hadn't thought out what I said at all. It was exactly how I felt.

"The children are very happy, too, Helen. They love you very much."

We planned to make the house a three-story house in the old tradition. On the first floor would be a room for Greg and Rusty, a room for Mike, a closet, a boys' bath, a study, and a library. On the second floor, level with the ground, we planned to have the carport, a laundry room, a family room, a room with probably Colleen, Rosemary, and Louise, and a bath near them. Then, across the hall, a room for Tommy and Nick and Gerry, and a bath across from their room. Then we would have a large living room.

We gave a lot of thought to the kitchen. We would have a six-burner stove in the center of the kitchen, surrounded by serving areas; a long kitchen table semicircled under the windows; plenty of sink space and storage space. We would have to have a large refrigerator, a double-oven stove, certainly a freezer. I planned, too, to have large storage bins in the kitchen for powdered milk, flour, and the most commonly used foods.

On the third floor we thought we'd have one large room for Veronica, Susan, Germaine, and Jean; another room for Janette, Mary, Joan, and Teresa. We wanted the youngest children to be closest to us. They would have their own bath. Then we would have our own room, bath, and dressing room.

It all sounded quite wonderful, but I still had some reservations. As I drove back to my house after one visit, I thought: Helen North, how could you get into this? You couldn't possibly be the mother of teen-agers even if they're very sweet. You shouldn't be getting yourself involved to this extent even if Frank were the most practical man in the world. And how practical can he be to plan such a marriage? I told myself all the things people were going to say to me later on: that it was a marriage entered out of loneliness; that it was a marriage of some convenience between Frank and me with little regard for the children; that it was a hasty marriage without enough thought and care. Yet I had considered all these things. I was the first to object to the idea of falling in love. I was the first to object to the idea of casting our lot together. I had the most serious objections to joining our families. And despite all this I knew it was the right thing.

I wrote to Dick's mother and father to tell them what I planned. They had always been the most considerate and gentle of people. They remained so. His mother wrote me a letter telling me that she wished I could bring to Frank the same happiness I had brought to Dick, and thanking me again for having brought such happiness into the life of her son.

I moved closer and closer to that incredible moment, the moment when I would become the mother of eighteen children, with the possibility of others coming later. And I felt immensely happy. I knew that I was in love with Frank. I was delighted by the reaction of my little ones to him and I was delighted by the attention his children showed me. Our love was as different from that first love for Dick as autumn is from spring. And yet it was rich in color, and vibrant and deep. It was a type of love that one might feel despite a great national disaster. It endured my own doubts and all the practical questioning of other people. It was an impossible love, and yet it had stood a test of reality which most loves would never be subjected to: the reality of joining together two very large families.

VIII

We saw each other almost every weekend, and it sometimes seemed as if we were spending most of our time running back and forth between San Leandro and Carmel. Our love grew during these meetings, which seemed always to be enriched by hilarity, joy, tenderness—all the strange combinations which fill the minutes of a couple in love.

What are my memories of those months? Working in my kitchen on a beautiful Sunday afternoon and overhearing Frank and six-year-old Phillip talking while Frank washed the car.

Frank asked, "Hand me that rag, Phil."

"That's not a rag. It's a towel."

"It's both; it's a towel and a rag."

"Can a thing be two things at the same time?"

"Yep."

There was a silence as Phillip pondered this. Then I heard Phillip press further. "Can a person be a person and a horse?"

"No."

"Then a thing cannot be two things at once."

"Your name is Phillip and you're a boy—right? That makes you two things at once, right?"

"Yep. My brother's name is Tommy and he's a boy. So he's two things at once."

"I said some things could be two things at once."

This was the talk that the boys loved and needed. It wasn't the kind of conversation a mother ordinarily encourages.

I remember sharply the July afternoon when Frank met Mother for the first time. I was apprehensive about it, so that before the meeting I joked with Frank about eloping. That really would have made a story: "PARENTS OF EIGHTEEN ELOPE."

My fears were groundless. Frank positively charmed Mother, but wisely he omitted mention of his ten children

47

during that first meeting. From then on, though, she was very anxious for me to "invite Frank over." She used this expression as if we all lived in a small town. Actually to "come over" Frank had to drive over a hundred miles. Mother seemed anxious to talk to me about Frank. I was reluctant because I was uneasy about concealing the fact of Frank's children from her. The poor woman thought my reluctance to talk about Frank showed a lack of interest.

"Helen, I'll talk to you frankly," she said. "I sensed Mr. Beardsley is seriously interested in you. He's an attractive man. He has nice manners and a good personality. These things count. Besides, Helen, it's not as if you had no responsibility, like Kay. You have those eight children to consider."

Kay would then speak right up. "That's right, Helen, believe me, not many men his age are willing to take on all this responsibility. Mother's perfectly right."

"Why don't you take Mother's advice yourself? Stop rejecting those proposals, Kay."

Mother interrupted. "Kay has plenty of time—"

"But she hasn't even married once. I'm a widow."

"But, Helen." Mother's voice contained an echo of a thousand admonitions, always given in a ladylike voice. "You may need help raising those children, and besides you're easily led."

Kay couldn't keep a straight face. It's amazing how a parent's impression of a child sometimes never changes. I had fallen in love and married young; therefore I was easily led. If we all lived another hundred years, I would never erase that impression.

I remembered reading a charming old novel of Cape Cod in which a minister's son is called "Sissy." He thereupon engages in a series of adventures all over the world, returns home twenty years later, and is still known in town only by his old nickname. One's role in the family sticks in somewhat the same way. Strange, how much I had lived in these years of love and travel and adventure, all of it unknown to my mother. The poor dear still worried about me as if I were very young.

I decided to tell Mother about Frank's children. I said quietly, "Mother, I have been concealing something from you. I intend to marry Frank."

"Excellent. Now you're showing some common sense."

"One other thing, Mother; he was married and lost his wife."

"Those things happen."

"And he has a family of ten children."

She was surprised only for a second, then I could see her recover her composure. "I told you he was a steady man. The family proves it. I think it's fine. Well, Helen, you do bring in some surprises."

"And I'm easily led."

"Easily led, yes." I went over and gave her a hug and a kiss. I loved her because of her incredible endurance, her manners and steadfastness to her ways and opinions in a swift-changing world. She didn't like emotional displays. But she said almost softly, "I don't quite understand all this, Helen, but I feel it's right. I'm not worried about you at all. And Mr. Beardsley is quite charming."

But the best times were the hours Frank and I shared. I learned much of Frank. He had put more thought into the bringing up of children than anyone I knew and read endless articles about their care. Some fathers actually kill themselves working to build financial security for their children, he felt, neglecting them in more important ways in order to store up riches for their future. Certainly it is important to work hard for your children, but if the only legacy you can give them is money it is a poor legacy indeed.

Frank thought childhood was a very short training period for adulthood. Too short. And the child needs each parent exactly when he needs him. When he needs a mother to confide some foolish, childish worry, he needs her then. When the child needs the father, he needs him. Children can't wait while the parent is busy establishing a far-away dream like financial security. A child doesn't measure a parent by adult rules. He measures him by childish rules. He measures him by his response to the child's need of the minute. The father may be planning great things for the son. He may work hard to have enough money to send the son to Harvard only to have the son leave high school partially because of the often absent parent. Frank was aware of the terrible human failing, the lack of communication from one generation to another.

We had both known good parents. Parents content to explain what the child wants to know. Content to keep pace with a child's slow-growing awareness. A parent restrained enough not to crowd too many ideas of good into a child's mind before he is ready. A parent ready to stand silently by childhood, with love as the bridge, to guide the children into maturity.

We talked of these things and our experiences with our children. Frank had an astonishing grasp of the role of the parent. Some of it came from his memories of his own parents; some from the life he shared with Fran. His experience in personnel work in the Navy may have been the key to the thought he put into sleeping arrangements, work assignments, playrooms for different age groups, constant thought and care that life in a large family would move effortlessly, with as little friction as possible.

Frank put it this way: "In personnel work we take a lot of care to make the best possible combinations of people working together. If we can apply the same care to running a large family, we'll cut down a lot of friction and make the house happier."

"I never thought of that. I'm always afraid I expect too much of the children. I feel like a scold at times."

"Just ask for reasonable co-operation. They'll come through."

By August, Frank and I had decided to be married the following year if we could work everything out. First on my list was a family conference to explain it all to the children.

They loved family conferences. They tumbled into the room speculating on the reason for the meeting. I said solemnly, "You have all met the Beardsley children. What do you think of them as brothers and sisters?"

Tommy was enthusiastic. "Boy, I'd have three big brothers. If anyone bothered Nick or the girls, all I'd have to do is call them. No one could wise off with us again."

Colleen said earnestly, "I'd love to have those kids for brothers and sisters."

I said, "Do you remember my telling you girls when we first moved into this house that I would never marry again?"

The girls nodded. The boys looked very surprised and pleased. It was a more important family conference than they had expected. Nicky said, "You wouldn't have to marry again. I mean, we'd just have them as brothers and sisters—"

Jean said, "No, Nicky."

I went on. "Something happened which I never could have foreseen. I met Mr. Beardsley. We fell in love and he wants me to marry him."

I was watching Janette. I could see the struggle in her mind. She wanted to enthuse like the others, yet she did not want to be disloyal to her dead daddy. I took her in my arms and looked into her eyes. "What do you think, Janette?"

50

She held me firmly. "I love my daddy in heaven, but I do want a daddy here on earth. And I do love Mr. Beardsley." She began to cry and hugged me.

The others took this as a signal all was settled. The questions tumbled from them. When would the wedding take place? Where? Would the Beardsleys move in with the Norths or would we move to their house? The boys were shouting their questions. I said firmly, "Hold it, now. We haven't made any decisions on a lot of these things."

Childlike, they were immediately disappointed. They hoped the marriage would take place the next day, or at least within a week. I told them it would most likely be the following year. They gave me the kill-joy look. Time to prepare is a gift of which youth seems neither aware nor appreciative. The fact they would have to wait many months for the fun and excitement of the wedding appalled them. Their attitude was: "Why is she talking about something so far away?" Another barrier between child and parent: a different perception of time. I gave each one a hug and sent him on his way. One worry was eliminated. The children approved.

It soon became evident that they more than approved.

One of the reasons that Frank and I had decided to marry the following year was that by then Frank's retirement pay would be increased, and at the same time all the contemplated changes in the house would be completed But both of us found ourselves being pressured by the children Frank's boys were aware that as soon as he was married their two little sisters would be back to live with them again: therefore they couldn't understand why there should be a delay. My own boys were anxious to be around their new "older brothers." Also, the constant commuting between San Leandro and Carmel began to become wearing. A few days after our decision a letter came to me from Frank's Rosemary. In it she wrote how much she and the other children wanted me to be their mother. The letter left me in tears. The pressure kept mounting in both families so that soon Frank and I began to feel wrong about delaying the inevitable. Finally, we yielded to both the pressure from the children and the demands of our own hearts. We decided to be married the following month, in September.

IX

Frank designed the wedding announcement:

Michael, Charles, Gregory, Rosemary, Louise,
Mary, Susan, Veronica, Germaine,
and Joan Beardsley
and
Colleen, Janette, Nicholas, Thomas,
Jean, Phillip, Gerald,
and Teresa North
Request the honor of your presence
at the marriage of their parents
HELEN BRANDMEIR NORTH
to
FRANCIS LOUIS BEARDSLEY
Saturday, the Ninth of September
Nineteen Hundred and Sixty-One
At Four O'clock in the Afternoon
Carmel Mission Basilica
Reception following
Copper Cup Room
U.S. Naval Postgraduate School

It was to be a simple wedding. The setting was beautiful, the Basilica of Carmel, one of California's original Spanish missions. Built by Padre Junipero Serra in 1770 on the Monterey Peninsula, it opens to the Pacific in a natural harbor. The mission and restored quadrangle are built on an elevation near the sea just south of Carmel on the road to Point Lobos. This location has been called "the most beautiful meeting of land and water in the world." The hills beyond are also beautiful. The building of the mission and the quadrangle, the location and completeness show the genius of Father Serra. For Monterey was to have been the capital of

52

California and this mission is located in the natural center of the peninsula.

It was a wonderful September day. We had received a dispensation from the diocese at Fresno, enabling us to be married at a 4 P.M. nuptial Mass. It gave us time to have the eighteen children dressed and ready for the ceremony. It also gave me time to become slightly nervous. Earlier, Kay had been with me while I got dressed in a green suit with a small mink collar. Kay was to be my maid of honor and was chattering a bit.

"Helen, you're not nervous?"

"Just slightly."

"Come on. What about the old Navy spirit?"

"I'm not nervous just for myself. I'm worried that one of the little Norths will ruin the whole wedding. When the priest asks if anyone knows any reason why this wedding shouldn't take place, one of mine, not one of Frank's, will say, 'Just a minute, Father. The Norths have to hold a family conference,' and Colleen, Janette, Nicky, and Tommy will all huddle right in the center aisle."

"Of course they won't, Helen. You'll be very proud of them. Anyhow they only say that in movies, I think."

"How do I look?"

"You look lovely."

"Do you think Bob will handle this all right?"

"Of course."

Bob was to give me away at the wedding. When Kay and I came downstairs, there was a good deal of confusion. Bob was in the living room looking at his watch. I had time to give Mother a hug before he hurried me out to the car. He drove us to the private entrance to the Mission Basilica.

There was a surprising crowd before the church. Naturally, the Navy had turned out—Frank's friends and shipmates, old friends of Dick and myself—as had relatives and sightseers. My dreams for a quiet wedding were shattered. I looked at Bob. He seemed aghast at the number of people.

We entered a small room off the main church. Inside, the organ was softly playing. Bob was still nervous. He made a brave attempt at humor. "You still have time to second-guess."

"No. I'm happy with the decision."

The sound of the organ ended abruptly. Then it blared forth imperatively. This was our cue. Bob looked resolute as I took his arm. We left the foyer and entered the main church.

The Basilica is small by modern standards, and its brown walls that reach high to the heavy-beamed ceiling made it seem narrow. I saw the pews crowded with family, friends, and neighbors. I still didn't see Frank. I walked forward a few steps and made a turn into the center aisle. Then I saw our children, who occupied the first row on both sides of the aisle—the boys scrubbed and shiny in new suits, and the girls in new white hats, white dresses, and white gloves.

It was a long aisle. Frank looked solemn but relaxed and confident. Father Geary, the chaplain, was on the altar, with Rusty and Gregory as servers.

Frank looked at me. I couldn't resist a little grin as I glanced at his best man. Larry Slattery, usually so bubbly, was grim as only a man uncomfortable in a stiff white collar can be. The children were watching me; for some reason the girls were solemn, while the boys wore wide grins. I took a few more steps and Bob placed my hand in Frank's. We stood together. Father Geary came over and we knelt before him. He recited the marriage exhortation, after which we arose and went through the familiar marriage ceremony. I thought, as the priest joined us in the marriage bond: Lord, make me strong enough and good enough to be worthy of this marriage.

After the blessing of the rings, Father Geary went on to read a marriage blessing from Psalm 127: ". . . Thy wife as a fruitful vine, on the sides of thy house."

I heard Kay cough. I did not dare look in her direction. There was a distant murmur in the church as the wits caught the line. I smiled despite my best intentions. Unawares, Father continued, " . . .Your children like olive plants around your table." From the first row a beacon of eighteen smiles flashed from our olive grove. Again I had the desire to smile, just like a child on a very solemn family occasion.

"May you see your children's children. Peace be upon Israel. Glory be to the Father and to the Son and to the Holy Spirit. Amen."

Now more familiar prayers followed. Perhaps because of my hard-bought experience in life, I was stunned not just by the beauty but by the humanity of the marriage service. The prayer to make us one in "the union of love and true affection," a prayer to unite our hearts "in the enduring bond of pure love," and the prayer that we "might be blessed in our children" followed one after another. They were prayers which rose from the deepest hopes of mankind. Now the

54

priest recited a prayer that the peace of Christ might dwell in our hearts, that we might have true friends, help those in need, be blessed in our work; and lastly a moving prayer that God might grant us "the harvest of a good life and a place in heaven."

We returned to our prie-dieu for the nuptial Mass. I was very moved by the prayers. It was as if I heard them for the first time with true inner awareness. I had borne the press of the years and the Biblical "heat of the day," and now I appreciated the depths of the plain human wants and needs that had gone into the prayers of the marriage ceremony.

The nuptial Mass began. There are prayers common to every Mass and special prayers for each occasion included in each individual service. For every wedding Mass the Epistle is from St. Paul and urges wives to be subject to their husbands. Did Frank glance at me with mock severity for an instant? I know when the words of the great apostle urged husbands to love their wives as their own bodies, I did glance at Frank for an instant with an attempt at sternness.

After the priest had said the Lord's Prayer, we again stood and knelt before him to receive the first part of the nuptial blessing. It sounded like a psalm. I remember the words: "Look with kindness on this thy servant who is now to be joined to her husband in the companionship of marriage. May the yoke that she is taking on herself be one of love and peace. May she be the beloved of her husband as was Rachel, wise as was Rebecca, long-lived and loyal as was Sarah."

We returned to our places. I was a little awed to be classed with these great Biblical figures. Yet that one prayer summed up everything I could hope to be as a wife.

At the end of the Mass, we received the last part of the nuptial blessing:

"May the God of Abraham, the God of Isaac, the God of Jacob be with you and may He fulfill in you His blessing so that you may see your children's children to the third and fourth generation."

As the prayers ended, I was asking God for the grace to live up to such a beautiful ceremony. Organ music poured through the Basilica. Frank and I turned toward each other. He was smiling. The children in the first pew were radiant with happiness. There was a spontaneous explosion of good feeling which seemed to radiate from that first bench throughout the Basilica.

Outside we stopped to have pictures taken. The Mission

55

grounds were even more crowded now, for along with the guests, friends, classmates of the children and well-wishers, the curious public waited, too. The national newspeople moved in on us with questions. We had become a "story" beyond anything either of us had imagined. They crowded around us, but Frank soon took my arm and led me to our car. He was smiling, but his grip was firm.

We drove south. Eleanor, one of Frank's six sisters, had bravely volunteered to take care of the children for the two weeks we would be gone. We drove without speaking. I think we shared a feeling of unreality. Our love and marriage were as much a miracle to us as the sun dying over the ocean, or the sunset-lit beauty of the Pacific coastline.

I broke the silence. "Do you think they'll be all right?"

"They'll really have a ball. It works out just about perfectly. The Norths are not in their teens. So my oldest will go all out to take care of them. Eleanor can handle anything. Anyhow, I'm confident my platoon system will work."

I let the assurance wash over me. It was such a comfort to have someone share the responsibility, the worries, the decisions. Especially, I thought, when it was as good a man as Frank.

We sped down the road before us, silent once more. I looked over at Frank. He turned and our eyes held for a moment.

He smiled. "You all right?"

I nodded. Yes, I was all right. And I felt almost like crying for the wonder of this new life that stretched before me. *Thank You, God,* I thought, *thank You for making everything all right.*

X

With eleven girls and seven boys in one house, how could we hope to avoid the quibbling that occurs when many lives are lived so close together? In the beginning I think the children were caught up in the excitement of the marriage. The whole affair was tremendously entertaining for them. The younger ones especially were enthralled by having a whole new set of brothers and sisters. Frank's oldest children were very happy for him. They had watched him all those long months and knew how he had suffered. They were so relieved that Frank had recovered: they would have been happy even if I had had fifteen children. They had worried, too, about Frank's two littlest ones whom he had placed with friends. Veronica and Jack Clipper, having no children of their own, had loved the babies dearly. There were times, Frank had told me, when, feeling he would never marry, he had thought about letting the Clippers raise them. Now their unit was together again, their father was happy, so what did it matter if eight more children were involved.

Tommy and Nicky naturally took to having older brothers. They strolled around the house, now imitating Mike, now Rusty or Greg. The littlest ones needed only the comfort of knowing they had parents who loved them.

The first signs of tension between the children arose between Rosemary and Colleen. It was very natural. They were both "little mothers" who had taken on responsibility far beyond their years. They were both conscientious about their work and their position in the family. The squabble arose because they were on a dish-washing detail together and Colleen felt Rosemary was not doing the dishes properly.

Rosemary very inelegantly called Colleen a "fink." Colleen's temper flared. More angry words were exchanged. This was no squabble between little girls over a toy or a TV program. I came into the kitchen and asked them both to be quiet. I could feel the tension in the room. Colleen had relaxed a bit, perhaps feeling that since I (her real mother) would now settle the problem she had little to fear. Rosemary was resolved not to retract anything. She was firm-jawed, her eyes flashing resentment.

I said, "All right, let's make a cup of tea and talk this over."

Both girls started to move to put on a kettle. Each stopped at the motion of the other. I said quickly, "I'll put on the water. You both sit down."

I sat with them. They carefully avoided each other's eyes.

"Now, tell me what this is all about."

Colleen said quickly, "She doesn't know how to wash dishes properly. That's all there is to it. Unless she doesn't care."

57

"I've been doing dishes very successfully since I was four years old and I don't need help from this know-it-all."

I had the feeling that the argument over the dishes was not the main issue, that the trouble was elsewhere. I told them this, that they were fighting about dishes, but something else was really bothering them. "Now, why are you angry with each other?"

They both looked at me. Rosemary said haltingly, "She's really too critical. After all, I'm nearly two years older than she."

Colleen said quickly, "One year and six months older."

"Rosemary, you think Colleen is too critical and doesn't give you the respect the difference in your age demands. Is that right?" Rosemary nodded and I turned to Colleen. "What do you think?"

"I think she's too bossy. I've taken care of a family too. She doesn't have to act so great."

I said a little prayer for guidance, then I said, "Colleen, when Rosemary's mother died, she had to be the mother of this whole house. So she knows a lot. And Rosemary knows how much help you have been to me with your younger brothers and sisters. You have more in common than you know."

They thought this over. They were reluctant to give up the dispute, as if, having finally broken their restraint and started to fight, they wanted to exploit it fully before each surrendered her advantage.

"O.K.," I said "You are both oldest girls in a family. You have more responsibility than anyone else. If you fight, the younger children could easily begin to fight. We might be in serious trouble."

They were both solemn. Naturally, pride held each girl a prisoner. I decided to try another approach.

"You have to pray that God will give you grace to avoid fights and have charity toward each other."

They both looked at me a bit uncertainly.

"You both know you have to pray for strength to do good."

They looked sheepish. Rosemary said, "Well, I always pray for big things."

"That's it," said Colleen. "I always pray for important things, too."

"It's very important that these families stick together, isn't it? Now, you two use your brains."

Colleen smiled a little ruefully.

"I guess I was too fussy about the old dishes."

Rosemary said quickly, "I'm sorry, Colleen; of course you're not a fink."

"So let's go back to work. O.K.?"

They were still not quite happy. Impulsively, Rosemary reached over and gave me a hug.

"I'm sorry now."

Quickly Colleen was at my other side. I hugged them both. I wanted to tell them they each faced a life of sorrows and joys, during most of which they would probably be far apart. Now they should take these good moments and enjoy each other. But I just hugged them. A parent has to be silent much of the time.

My role as a mother of teen-age boys rested lightly on me at first. The boys were gentlemen and didn't seem affected with all the problems of which I had heard. Just before they were to go back to school, Greg talked with me privately. Usually ready with a quick smile and fast wit, Greg was serious this time.

"Listen, Mom, I thought I'd better check out something about Mike with you."

"What is it, Greg?"

"I hate to bring it up, but I know Mike is worried. There's this girl, a real drag on anybody. She's got Mike all tied up in a knot."

"How, Greg?"

"It's all one way, don't get me wrong. She has a crush on him. He's only dated her twice and she's got the word all over town that they're going steady."

"But, Greg, this isn't so serious. What if she does say they're going steady? Mike can simply say they're not."

Greg was very earnest.

"He won't. He's too good a guy, know what I mean? He'd be embarrassed for her. The girls in this school are death on this. If you're going steady, no one else will go out with you. Listen, Mom, the girls run that whole school like the Gestapo or something."

I had to smile at Greg's earnestness. I remembered that when I was in high school I wanted to be free to date different fellows. I didn't understand this new fad, but I didn't want Greg worried.

"Greg, thanks. I'll see if I can help Mike."

"I don't want him to think I'm butting into his affairs."

"Of course not, Greg."

I wondered why Mike didn't discuss this with me himself. Perhaps he didn't feel free enough with me yet. Or, worse, he didn't have confidence in me as a mother. I wanted to give him a chance to talk with me. I was astonished at how much the younger boys had come to depend on him.

A day or so later Mike and I were alone in the kitchen and he started to discuss Greg's topic with me.

"Mom, what's your idea on this going steady?"

It was such a wonderfully roundabout question that I smiled. Before I could answer, Nick came into the room holding a plastic aircraft carrier.

"Mike, can you help me just with this superstructure?"

"Sure," said Mike. "Did you follow instructions on the rest?"

"Right down the line," said Nick proudly.

Mike turned to me. "I'll just check this out for him. O.K., Mom?"

I nodded, not wanting to embarrass him. The same sort of thing happened several times during the next few days. Finally, when the youngsters were swimming, I had a chance to speak to Mike.

"You asked me about steady dating the other day, Mike."

"Well, I guess I did. I just wanted your slant on it."

"When I was dating the most popular girls avoided steady dating in high school."

He seemed a bit doubtful. "I guess so, but now all the girls want to go steady. To tell you right out, my problem is there is a girl who says we're going steady."

"Did you ask her to go steady?"

"No. I just took her out twice. I don't get it. She's pretty and everything, but I didn't ask her to go steady."

"Who is she, Mike?"

"A girl in my class, Pat Truxler. I can't very well say out and out that she's wrong. I don't want to hurt her feelings."

"That's very kind of you, Mike. But this girl could ruin your social life at school."

"Well, yes, that's right. But if I say we're not going steady I embarrass her, and if I say we are, I lie and cut off all the other girls."

"Mike, this takes a form of courage, too. You just have to have the courage to explain to the girl you didn't intend to go steady. If you act as if it is just a misunderstanding, you

60

won't hurt her pride. You have to cut a thing like this off, Mike. There's no halfway surgery."

"O.K., Mom, I'll give it a try."

A week passed before Mike spoke about his problem again.

"You were right about that girl, Mom. I'm glad I asked you."

"Did it work out O.K.?"

He shook his head and grinned. "As well as it could, I guess. If it had gone any further that girl would have been buying a wedding gown."

We didn't speak of it again, but I was glad that Mike had asked my advice on something so delicate. It meant he really considered me his mother.

XI

No amount of imagination could have prepared Frank and me for the enormous quantities of food, clothing, and everything else that a family of twenty would consume. Budgetwise, we knew that we would be able to manage. What we underestimated was the actual physical job involved in shopping for a family of twenty. A gallon of jam, 60 pounds of oatmeal, 14 dozen eggs, a box of apples, 50 loaves of bread, 100 pounds of potatoes, 60 pounds of powdered whole milk, 54 pounds of hamburger, 14 heads of lettuce—all would be lugged into the house and quickly disappear. During an ordinary breakfast the children would consume nearly forty pieces of toast, a gallon of fruit juice, a gallon of milk, six quarts of hot cereal, and three dozen eggs.

Eventually Frank and I found that making up a shopping list for supplies of this magnitude was almost completely useless. We decided that the best procedure would be a general scrutiny of the market shelves. This way we could select what we needed as we went along, making sure we got enough to last at least a week.

On our very first shopping trip, Frank and I didn't know

this, however. Very offhand about the whole thing, we started off for the Navy commissary like any other happy newly married couple. Anyone who knows the Navy commissary will tell you that this is the best time to go there—when you're feeling gloriously happy and deeply satisfied with life. For the commissary is short on just about everything that counts: aisle space, help, ample shopping carts, and large-sized cans of food.

Before we left, I thought of taking some of the children with us to help out, but then decided that Frank and I could easily handle two baskets each. This was our first mistake. With Frank in the lead, we started down the first aisle, each of us pulling and pushing our baskets. Our intention was to work each side of the aisle, checking with each other as we went along. In this way, we thought, we could put a curb on each other's spree-buying tendencies and also shop in half the time. We hadn't been in the first aisle for more than half a minute when we realized traffic was piling up behind us and people were beginning to complain. On top of this, everybody who came toward us with a cart took one look at our line-up and backed down the aisle. In the Navy commissary the same rules apply to the aisles as apply to a one-car road when two cars meet: the one that's gone more than halfway when they meet has the right of way. So when you meet an oncoming cart you just hope you're more than halfway.

I knew how the people in back of us felt: to get behind two people with four carts was tragic. I became so embarrassed that I found myself tempted to add to the murmurs of discontent behind me. At one point I wanted to tap Frank on the shoulder and say, "Pardon me, sir, but if you must shop for your two-week camp-out with your Boy Scout troop, why don't you go to a supermarket?"

Each time we came to the end of the aisle where there was space to maneuver and pass, we stopped and pretended to reconnoiter while we let people go by. It helped, but not much. Sometimes the grumbling behind us got really loud when people came to a shelf only to find that the Beardsleys had completely emptied it. The range of comments on us and our four baskets was wide.

". . . stocking a bomb shelter."

"Two to one they're shopping for civilian pals."

"Maybe they have a lot of kids."

"Nobody has that many kids."

At Soaps, Detergents and Toilet Tissues, Frank went to get

two more baskets. There are five bathrooms in our house and a washer-drier that stops running only on holidays. I heard one man offer his companion six to five that we ran a boarding house.

Finally, exhausted from pushing and pulling six carts, we stood in line at one of the cash registers. Our high-wire act had taken an hour and a half, but it still wasn't over.

While I waited in line, Frank got two large cardboard boxes from a clerk, filled them with forty-nine loaves of bread and pushed them up to the check-out counter. Now everyone was watching us. Mercifully, I was busy putting our purchases on the moving conveyor.

The cashier must have checked out five hundred separate items. When he hit the key with a flourish to tabulate the total, it rang up to $127.33. The tape from the register was over six feet long. The box boy worked furiously for more than twenty minutes loading the order into bags.

At the parking lot, Frank and the boy labored to find a place for all the bags in the car. Then we both sat in the front seat—exhausted. Frank said wearily, "There must be an easier way."

There was. But we didn't find it for some time. I had originally thought that shopping for a family of twenty would be just a bit more complicated than shopping for nine. But it was far more involved than that. Eventually I found out that what was necessary was a pattern of shopping completely different from the average family's. But until I learned this I had to go through more than one baptism of fire.

One memorable skirmish occurred when I had to take the children to buy school outfits. Ordinarily I would not have taken them all at once, but school was opening in a few days and I had little choice. One morning as Frank was leaving for work, I told him that I was going to take all the children out to buy shoes. Almost late, he was in a hurry.

"You think you can manage it?"

"Why not?" I said naïvely.

He gulped his coffee and headed for the door. "Go late in the afternoon," he said. "There'll be fewer people around."

Good advice, I thought. I called Kay and she took the afternoon off. I decided she would drive her car and I would drive ours and we'd do the most efficient job of shoeing a family the world had ever seen.

It all started out wonderfully. Kay was on time and took eight of the oldest in her car. This left me with ten in the

station wagon. We drove off. I had still not become accus-
tomed to the sympathetic smiles, the winks and nods, the
aloof, disapproving frowns from other drivers that met us at
traffic lights. Later, I was to enjoy such encounters, nodding
and winking back at the big-family approvers and looking
properly harassed for the frowners' edification. I kept within
sight of Kay. The children were trying to promote a race;
they were disappointed to be following her car. Janette sat at
my elbow.

"You could have taken her at the last light. We're only
going thirty-five; let's go, huh, Mom?"

"We're just going to buy school clothes, Janette; we're not
in a race."

"But couldn't we get there first?"

"Maybe we will. Let Mother drive."

We finally reached the store. Inside, as Kay and I herded
our eighteen toward the children's department, a voice said in
a dulcet tone, "My, what a well-behaved class."

"We're not a class, we're a family," Rusty piped up.

The owner of the voice, a rather tight-suited individual
who smelled of cologne, smiled. He looked at Kay. "Are they
all yours?"

"No." Kay smiled back at him.

"I didn't think so."

Kay pointed at me. "They're all hers."

People had begun to look our way. I was getting embarrassed. To make matters worse, one of the boys chose that
moment to sing out innocently and indignantly, "How come
he's wearing women's perfume?"

The children moved closer to him, as he tried to pretend
they were not there. He didn't make it. Crimson-faced, he
said, "May I help you?"

Crimson-faced, I answered, "Yes, where's the shoe department?"

"I'll escort your little party over. Follow me."

Kay, of course, was enjoying the whole thing. And as we
were led to the shoe department she glanced over at me and
said, "Smile, you're on Candid Camera."

I made a face at her, envying her enjoyment. Kay has almost always had trouble with long, serious ceremonies, even
church services. Solemn speeches send her into a panic. She
always seems to see some incongruity no one else does and
can't control her mirth. Unfortunately, we're built differently
in that respect. So while Kay marched along, hard put to

keep from laughing, I found myself pretending I was not a part of this department store safari at all. I hoped people would assume I just happened to be walking in the same direction. Our guide dropped us at the shoe department, threw us an agonized smile, and ran off.

Fortunately, the shoe department salesman had no peculiarities that the children could call attention to. A big bear of a man, he was patient and competent, and the children reacted by taking the whole thing very seriously. But in spite of this the actual physical job of fitting them all was incredible. Those who were going to the Mission School got white saddle shoes, which were part of their uniforms. These were not too hard to select. The salesman began measuring the little ones' feet and getting shoes for them to try on. And while they did this, he was measuring other feet and getting other shoes, and then rushing to measure the older boys' feet.

Slowly the stacks of shoe boxes grew, and I marveled at the fantastic number of shoe sizes that must have been floating around in the salesman's head: men's sizes for the older boys; from a six to a twelve in children's shoes; from a one to a three in girls' shoes; from a six to a ten in ladies' shoes, which the older girls wore. Besides all the mental work of lengths, and widths to consider from double A to quadruple D, he had the tremendous job of juggling all those boxes as he made his way from the floor to the stockroom and back again. Unfortunately for the poor man, while I was trying to help Louise, who has trouble getting exactly the right fit, the youngsters had decided to pass shoes back and forth among each other and to try on each other's shoes. Kay was trying to handle this diplomatically, which meant that she was encouraging rather than discouraging; and to add to the sensation of imminent chaos, a curious crowd had begun to gather.

One round, fat little man began a discussion on large families with Mike, while a woman in a black cloth coat and a little flowered hat tried to give me a few words of advice on raising children. A gray-haired gentleman who claimed he was a retired shoe salesman seemed bent on getting in the way of our shoe salesman, giving him advice on handling a large number of customers at the same time.

The whole procedure took over an hour, and by the time it was over various employees had joined the onlookers and stood by making suggestions, while an increasing number of children also stood staring—drawn, as their parents were, out of pure curiosity. I had made sure that Colleen, Rosemary,

65

Mike, Rusty, Greg, Janet, Louise, and Mary were fitted. I hated even to look over at Kay and the little ones. I had the distinct feeling that things had not gone right in her section, for now her face had taken on the harried look it generally did if things didn't work out the way she had planned.

At one point she and the salesman got into a heated discussion over the fit of Veronica's shoes. Kay was insisting that she should be able to feel the toe and he was insisting that the toes didn't matter, that it was the fit of the ball of the foot that counted. I caught her eye. She was exasperated. I grinned demonically. "Smile," I said, "you're on Candid Camera."

When we finally got all the shoes in packages and up to the counter, I was a little dismayed to have to write out a check for $156—plus tax. Of course, we had budgeted the money, but still it was an awful lot of cash for one hour's shopping, just to buy the children one pair of shoes apiece.

I was in the kitchen when I heard Frank's car ease into the carport that evening. I envisioned him walking in and asking me how the shopping trip went. Why, just fine, Frank, I was prepared to say. Instead of coming right in, though, he started kicking the door with his foot. "Hey, somebody, open up!" he yelled.

I opened it and there stood Frank holding a mountain of sneakers. Rushing past me, he barely made it to the table, where he tumbled his burden. Straightening up, he beamed at me, then pointed to his hoard.

"Just looka that, will you?"

"Supper, I presume, is served. Where'd they come from?"

"The Navy Exchange. Helen, there was such a fantastic sale on them I couldn't pass it up."

I didn't know what to say.

"Honey, if we don't use them now we will eventually, don't you see?"

"How about the sizes?"

"I didn't have much time. I just told them to mix me up twenty pairs from six to twelve." My disappointment must have showed, for Frank hastened to reassure me. "Helen, if some don't fit we can exchange them. But don't you see? Eventually they've got to fit someone!"

As things turned out, twelve out of the twenty fit someone perfectly.

We soon came to realize that this was the key to our shopping problem. Instead of doing as other families did, buying generally what there was an immediate foreseeable need for, we found that by buying more than we needed we could save an enormous amount of money in the long run. In other words, we found that not only was it a waste of time for us to shop as other families do, but it cost us more money to do so. Time after time we saved money by buying shirts, socks, underwear, blouses—anything that was on special sale. This also applied to food.

Each time a local market features a "loss leader" for the week, we buy a case lot. The result is that we have special storage closets for everything. When one of the children needs a new shirt he simply goes to the shirt closet; shoes he can generally find in the shoe closet. Naturally, we still take the children out to buy clothes on the spot for them, but the majority of the youngsters' needs can be met from our own storage closets. Thus it probably costs us much less than the average family to clothe and feed each child.

We also learned how to save time in sorting the countless clothes that went into the washer. In lieu of using a hamper, we took our cue from the post office. As clothes are soiled they're put into the proper cubbyhole, so that when they're washed and dried there's no identification problem. Time is saved in matching up socks by using white ones as much as possible.

As I think back now, I can remember that Frank and I thought at first that our biggest problem would be knitting the two families together well. But as things turned out this took second place to the actual job of organizing the household so that it ran as smoothly as any other. Sometimes when I look at our present comfortable and well-run home, I wonder that I could have made all the mistakes I did. But I imagine everyone feels this way. It took us some time to learn the easy way to do things.

Every time I remember that first trip for shoes, I have to laugh. Frank did ask me later how it had gone.

"Fine," I told him.

I've made mistakes, but one thing I have learned is that it's not necessary to tell the poor man every last detail of a shopping trip when he comes home from work, especially if it was anything like the shoe-buying excursion.

XII

Less than a month after our marriage, Frank and I received a note from a Mr. Cleaver of the home economics department of a well-known university, asking if he could interview us for a paper he was writing. We thought this might be fun. I remember feeling very proud of the wonderful ideas Frank had to make our family work. I wrote an immediate invitation for Mr. Cleaver to visit us.

He came one Saturday morning. The little ones alerted me that a man was walking up our hill. A few minutes later, Mr. Cleaver introduced himself. He was a young man well over six feet tall. I must have stared at him. He shifted uncomfortably. "I had an appointment to visit your home," he said.

How could I have made the appointment on a Saturday? But I had. I invited him inside. He had the awestruck attitude of a disciple meeting Gandhi. He quickly put down an attaché case and drew out a notebook.

"Dr. Wagner, my home economics professor, recommended I do this study." Even as he spoke his eyes were fascinated by the six-burner stove in the center of the kitchen, the double ovens, the huge refrigerator, the built-in breakfast nook. He brought his attention back to me by sheer will power.

"You are, in effect, Mrs. Beardsley, the soldier in the field, and we at the university are the armchair generals."

"I don't feel that military—"

"No, no, of course not. I have some questions that are very personal. If you'd rather not answer them, very well. But it would give us at the university a more complete picture to project from."

"You are from the home economics department?"

"Of course. I have all sorts of questions. Just to ask a personal one, what is your budget to maintain this home? Please don't hesitate to refuse to answer, although it will go in the study under a file number."

"I don't mind answering if you wouldn't mind asking the questions in the laundry. I'm matching up socks. It will probably take me all afternoon. I will have to match perhaps seventy-five pairs."

Mr. Cleaver was delighted by the figure; he made a careful note of it. It was almost as if he had made an important scientific finding. Strange, how easily the most extraordinary situation had become ordinary to us. I smiled to think what a mine of statistics this home would yield to Mr. Cleaver.

When we reached the laundry, I answered the question. "Our total monthly family income is $1428. Frank's Navy pay, including all allowances, amounts to $894. The remaining $534 comes to my children in Social Security and dependents' benefits."

"Do you have a budget?" Mr. Cleaver was lefthanded, and there was an extraordinary amount of armflopping to record each fact in his notebook.

"Yes, a payment for the mortgage, $250 a month; property taxes, phone, utilities are $155; insurance, $126; church and schools, $36; clothing, $50; food, $450. The total budget expenses are $1142 a month."

"Amazing," said Cleaver. "I wouldn't have thought you could feed a family on, let me see"—he figured in his pad— "sixty-six cents a day for each person."

"We do. We have to shop very carefully."

"Of course. Is Mr. Beardsley an engineer?"

"No, he's a career Navy man."

"Everything seems so organized. You a home economics major in college?"

"No, I studied nursing."

I suspected some of Mr. Cleaver's pet hopes were fading. I think he envisioned a society of engineers, with home economics majors as wives, marching bravely toward tomorrow. Which was fine with me, if they figured out some way to match up socks easily.

"Do you mind, Mrs. Beardsley, if I look over the arrangements of your house?"

"Not at all. This is general cleaning day. You'll find some very busy children all over the house."

"Then you don't have any expenses for maid service, cooking, ironing, cleaning, janitor work . . . ?"

"That's right. Nor can we afford big birthdays, allowances, cars for our children, insurance to guarantee them an effortless life. We can only give them our care and time and love."

69

"Unfortunately, I can't enter those things in my notebook."

"Then love isn't part of home economics? Or sacrifice or devotion?"

"Mrs. Beardsley, I'm all for those things, truly I am. But I have no blocks or squares to rate these things."

With an awkward gesture he showed me a form he had. He was right. I guess no one considered these virtues in theory. Yet they could make the difference between a happy meal and a sad one; between a loving family and a divided one.

I matched the socks while Mr. Cleaver, whom I had entrusted to Greg, explored the house. He returned sixty-eight pairs of socks later. He had diagrammed each room of the house and made a neat balance sheet of the budget figures I had given him. I was about to ask if we had passed inspection when Frank came in with Mike. Without doubt, Frank is pleased that his house works. The design is his; and the fact that it operates well is also to Frank's credit. He quickly gave Mr. Cleaver a window on the "logistics" of the situation. I heard them discuss the advantage of buying non-fat powdered milk (we saved $15 per month over liquid non-fat milk), the advantage of buying eggs by fifteen dozen lots.

I guess fate had made Frank a home economist without benefit of degree. In any event, Cleaver was intrigued by his opinions. He said enthusiastically, "This house is great, not just for home economics. Think of what the psychology boys would do with all those siblings. Or the sociologists with the social frame of reference for eighteen children. A great study. Home economics just scratches the surface. The business school could do a management study here, and the school of journalism—"

Frank put a hand on his sleeve, "Mr. Cleaver, why not just let this be our secret, the home economics people and the Beardsleys?"

"Of course, Mr. Beardsley. I get the strangest feeling the prof sent me here on a hunch, just to see if I could raise the biggest question of all."

"What question?" Frank asked seriously.

"This question your wife brought up. I think he sent me here to find out what place love and devotion have in home economics. I had all the formula but that. Now I don't know."

He shrugged in such an awkward, tall, shy man's way, that Frank and I both grinned. It is comforting to know there are professors so close to the practical. Frank opened a Coke and offered it to Mr. Cleaver, who declined it. He looked at Frank owlishly. "I still can't imagine how it works. I can see that the figures balance. I believe that home management is just as important as business management, but personally I wonder what happens first thing in the morning?"

"On a school day?" Frank asked.

"Well, yes!"

"Morning breaks on our eight bedrooms. All twenty of us tumble out of bed. Mike, our oldest boy, takes charge of making lunches. He makes about twenty-five peanut butter and jelly sandwiches on the kitchen counter. Rusty makes a pot of oatmeal, using a whole box of it each morning. Rosemary prepares the orange juice, using four cans of concentrate. Tommy and Nick set the table for twenty—you can see it's banquet size." Frank looked at me.

"I sound the alarm and check the bedrooms for stragglers," I went on. "Louise runs the diaper detail. She changes Joan and Teresa. Colleen has the responsibility of checking Susan, Veronica, and Janette to make sure their beds are made and their room is picked up. Greg helps Phillip and Gerald get dressed."

I paused. Cleaver had stopped taking notes. I think that the names had stunned him. It was one thing to write down a number, but to realize these were eighteen little people was quite different.

Frank finished his Coke. "Don't forget the equipment detail. Mary and Jean check to see that everyone has pencils, erasers, and school equipment. Germaine helps too. Who does that leave?"

"You, Mr. Beardsley."

"Me?" Frank laughed. "I eat a very quick breakfast and go to work like any other father."

Cleaver checked his list carefully. He said, "I don't suppose you have any tax problem with this number of dependents?"

"Right," Frank said. "I can't afford a big trust fund to guarantee these children a college education, but when they're ready to go we'll get them through in one way or another. We're not a rich family, but we are a saving one. Besides, I don't think there have ever been more or better opportunities for scholarships, grants, and loans than there are today."

"I agree with you, Mr. Beardsley. I'm on a California State Scholarship."

It seemed impossible, but Mr. Cleaver actually looked like a 6'6" version of Wally Cox. He continued to make marks in his notebook. "You have no provision for medical insurance or medical expenses."

"That's one special dividend from the service. Our medical expenses are covered. This is very important; without it, a serious illness of just one of the children would put that budget out of commission entirely."

"Does it have any drawbacks?"

Frank hesitated for just a second. Then he said, "Navy doctors can set a broken bone as well as anyone, but I think we lose something by not having a steady family doctor. A doctor who knows a family's health history has a lot going for him. Navy doctors, like the rest of us, are often transferred. They leave complete records, but I think there is nothing like a doctor who knows you personally and knows what illnesses run in a family."

"But you receive all the proper laboratory procedures, medicine, technical studies?"

"Yes, that part is wonderful. If you ever need an x-ray, a blood transfusion, or a special drug, it's there. Once when Greg was suspected of having a heart ailment I saw eight doctors in conference on his case. Fortunately, he was all right."

"So first-class treatment is available when you need it?"

"I don't think we could do without it. How many times does a serious prolonged illness wipe out the savings of the average family? Imagine what it would do to us."

Mr. Cleaver stood up. "Well, I guess that covers everything. I know the question my wife will ask me: 'How does it actually work?' My answer will be that the home is organized. The children don't just live here but they are a creative part of the family. And I'll tell her the Beardsleys are the most creative parents I know."

"Creative?" Frank asked with a smile. "Mr. Cleaver, you're putting us on."

He blushed. "No, no. I didn't mean the number of children you have. I should have said imaginative."

The interview ended on that note. I didn't know whether we were more imaginative than most parents, or whether just having this many children made you imaginative very quickly.

XIII

By fall I knew that I was expecting a baby. At first I told myself it just wasn't so, even while I felt a mixture of curiosity and excitement about it. I told myself it was almost impossible to be the mother of eighteen children and still be very curious about Number Nineteen, but I was. I thought: Helen Beardsley, anyone would think you'd be more than satisfied to settle down with eighteen children and not complicate matters by having another. I couldn't help but imagine the letters that would come from irate taxpayers and "ban the baby" groups all over the country, expressing their indignation over the Beardsleys' having still another child. At the same time I wondered how the children would react. I waited a few days to be quite certain before I told Frank. One night after he had come home from work, he settled down with a cocktail. He had offered me one, but I said no.

"Well," Frank said, "nice and quiet tonight, isn't it?" Faint sounds of the children could be heard from different parts of the house.

"No more than usual," I replied.

He took a sip of his cocktail, savoring it. "Maybe it only seems quieter because I'm getting used to it."

"Don't get too used to it. It might not last."

"It'll last, all right. I'm amazed sometimes at how well the children have worked out with each other, better than we ever could have expected. I'm proud of them." He smiled and leaned back comfortably in his chair. "And proud of you, too. I'll tell you," he said wistfully, "sometimes I think I don't deserve all this quiet happiness."

"You deserve the happiness, but I'm not so sure about the quiet."

"I don't think I understand that cryptic remark."

"I just wondered if you didn't think things were becoming a bit dull?"

"Heavens, no. We've just settled down from a whirlwind

courtship, a hectic wedding. We've just rearranged the house so that it's perfectly engineered to efficiently fulfill the needs of a family of twenty. No, no, it's not dull at all."

He took a sip from his drink and looked at me closely.

"You don't mean that you're finding this life dull?"

"Of course not. Actually, I feel more energy here than I had in San Leandro. I don't have nearly as much difficulty with the house or the children. My nerves are better. And I have you."

"So how did this discussion start?"

"I merely suggested that things are perhaps a bit quiet for us. I mean, we lead more hectic lives than most people do."

"And what do you expect will change this serenity?"

" 'Expect' is the word."

"You mean . . . ?"

"Yes."

"Have you seen the doctor?"

"I never do until I'm a lot further along, but I'm sure."

He was touchingly happy. I suppose a sensitive man is always moved at the prospect of a new life emerging from his love. And he was as excited as if he had never had a child before.

"This is really great. I'm so happy and so in love, we had to have a child."

"You're really very nice, Frank."

"Do you have any idea when, I mean so we can do some planning?"

"I said, "About the middle of July."

"You feel all right now? I mean, you're not sick or anything?"

"I feel fine . . ."

"You look awfully serious all of a sudden," he said.

"I don't mean to. But I just thought about the Rh factor."

Both Dick and I and Frances and Frank had faced each birth with the shadow of the Rh factor hanging over us. I had almost dismissed it from my mind, seeing eighteen healthy children. But once I knew I was pregnant, the old worries revived. Frank asked, "Do you think they have something new on that business?"

"I'll check with the doctor and find out."

Years ago the women's magazines carried stories of the Rh factor in childbirth almost every month. If an Rh-negative mother bears a child with an Rh-positive father, the newborn baby may suffer from jaundice and a condition of the blood

74

which could kill the baby or permanently damage his brain. The alternative is a drastic series of blood transfusions begun at birth. The condition is frightening because the possibility of the child's inheriting such a condition increases with each successive pregnancy. There's no doubt that our percentage of healthy babies was clearly against medical expectancy. But on the other hand, I did have the reassurance of eighteen healthy children. I knew that the condition was serious enough for any doctor who had seen thousands of stillbirths and mentally defective children resulting from such pregnancies to be worried. But there is no longer the same air of panic about the Rh factor as there formerly was.

We decided not to tell the children right away but to have a family picnic soon and then tell them about the brother or sister who would be common to all of them. We became excited at this idea. It sort of added to the union of the whole family that this little tot would be the one who was not stepsister or step-brother, but would be actually a product of our love.

After dinner that night I checked the workroom downstairs, where the boys were busy with their homework. Frank had provided excellent encyclopedias. It was almost a small library, where the older boys could work. I checked the little ones, too. Then Frank and I went upstairs to our room.

With the lights out there is a beautiful view of the hills of Carmel. It is one of my favorite times of night—when I know the children are asleep or nearly asleep, when Frank has relaxed and I can look out from our bedroom and see the cars moving along the road at the bottom of the hill on which our house is built. I can see the lights on in our neighbors' houses and the eternal stars in the sky.

Looking out the window on this night, knowing there was new life within me, I could only wonder at the immensity of existence, the pale moon, the distant stars, the cold silence between planets. What did it mean?

I think I heard the car before I saw it, a new, sleek sports car speeding around the curve at the bottom of the hill, tires screeching. I looked down in time to see it fail to make the turn and crash into a pole across from our house. It was so sudden. There was the crash and then the silence. Then I heard a girl's voice.

"Larry, I'm hurt, Larry, I'm hurt."

I went to the phone to call the police. Frank had been asleep. The crash woke him up. I heard in the distance the sound of a police ambulance. I told Frank what had happened and we went back to the window. Then he began getting dressed to go downstairs and see what he could do to help. Greg and Rusty were already heading down the driveway. Now people were coming from the houses at the bottom of our hill. The girl's screams continued. No sound came from the boy who had been driving.

I said to Frank, "I don't think there's any need to go down now. The ambulance sounds very close."

He said, "Those poor kids . . . Didn't you go to sleep at all?"

"No, I was standing here, just thinking and looking out at the stars. Then that car came around the bend and went out of control."

Frank didn't say anything. We both looked down now from the window which had been such a delight to both of us. The ambulance and police cars arrived in a remarkably short time, but the car had hit the pole in such a way that the boy, pinned and unconscious behind the wheel, could not be gotten out without first dragging away the Jaguar. They had to call a tow truck. There was a wait. Red lights flashed. People stood around—the ambulance crew, the police, the neighbors, our own boys—and above everything the girl's voice continued to shrill. She was still calling Larry.

Finally the tow truck arrived and pulled the wreck off the pole enough so that they could pry the boy loose from his seat to put him in the ambulance. I later learned that the boy had never regained consciousness and the girl, too, had died in the hospital.

I was struck again with the terrible suddenness of death and with the idea that I held life within me and life was precious and shouldn't be wasted on fast cars and sharp turns, on wars and preparing for wars. Life should never be wasted. I had always had enormous respect for life, but just seeing death suddenly striking at the bottom of our street had renewed my reverence. I was glad the Beardsleys were going to have another baby. I thought: Lord, there are degrees of excellence in the service to mankind. Most people would agree that the birth of an Einstein, a Bergson, a Pasteur, a Curie, would be worth any suffering. I agreed with this, too. I would hesitate to prevent a great man of science from living, although no great scientists have appeared in our families.

I think of these scientists as finding a part of the truth, the startling, wonderful bits of truth. All truth comes from the

Holy Spirit and there are some souls to whom it is given to grasp great truths: these are the mystics, the saints, or even simple men or women of truth. To prevent one of them from living or to have one die is a senseless thing. The body crushed against the telephone pole was, to me, a great crime against humanity.

I tried to remember this so that I would have an answer for the next person who asked me: "Do you really think you can afford to have another child?"

"I don't know if I can afford not to," I would say.

XIV

In line with our decision to announce the news of the new baby to the children at a family outing, one Sunday we packed a picnic lunch. "Lunch" consisted of forty sandwiches, thirty bananas, two dozen apples, twenty dill pickles, and three gallons of root beer. It was a beautiful day. We decided to drive to the Santa Cruz mountains.

We enjoyed doing things in a group. Some families have loners who cut themselves off from the rest, find their own pursuits and pleasures. We don't happen to have any loners. The idea of a family picnic delighted the children. It had taken all of the girls working at top speed over an hour just to get the food ready, but it was a holiday for them, even to help. Janette had charge of the dill pickles, taking them from the small half-barrel in which we stored them and wrapping them in aluminum foil.

I listened to the flow of the girls' talk. Rosemary asked Colleen, "Do you think Daddy would like a special sandwich all of his own? Sort of a Dagwood? We can make it."

"That's a neat idea. We'll make him a special submarine sandwich."

I smiled to myself, hoping that Frank had a good appetite. Now, along with making the forty sandwiches—twenty bologna and twenty peanut butter and jelly—the girls were making Frank his submarine sandwich.

I heard Janette say: "I'll slice one of these dill pickles lengthwise. So it covers all the bread."

Jean was in charge of hard-boiled eggs. "I put on two extra for Daddy's submarine."

From what I could gather after listening to suggestions from Jean and Louise, Frank was to be faced with a monumental French roll of a sandwich with bologna, salami, ham, eggs, pickles, French dressing, mustard, two kinds of cheese. I heard Germaine add: "I know where there's a dead goldfish we could use."

Then Veronica: "Oh, no, you don't eat fish."

Susan chimed in. "You eat some fish, cooked. Maybe if we cooked your goldfish, Germaine, we could put it in Daddy's sandwich."

Rosemary said, "Susan, you take Germaine and Jean and check your room."

I was glad the discussion on the goldfish was ended, but the construction of the sandwich went on. Mary said positively, "I think it needs something more. I know, a dash of rosemary."

They had wrapped the submarine sandwich in aluminum foil and put it in the oven. Now they were busy with the rest of lunch. I was feeding Teresa and Joan during the kitchen preparations, and suddenly I thought about the announcement that was to come. I hugged Teresa to me, the little girl who had drawn me to life when life had been so harsh. Each child has a special place in a parent's heart, and Teresa had this meaning for me.

Mike came in holding a football.

"It's the season, so I'm bringing this. You haven't seen Dad punt. I'm telling you, it's something!"

The girls were now conspiratorially making a special lunch for me. Louise was making very delicate sandwiches, cutting off the crusts. It was strange how dainty they all seemed to think I was. I got only two slices of pickle. They didn't know I was eating for two, as people said in the old days. I was in great appetite; I would probably end up eating a portion of Frank's incredible sandwich as well as my own.

The boys were busy bringing the equipment and loading the cars. Frank emerged from our room sporting a very jaunty baseball cap, a sweatshirt, tennis shoes, and his "golfing pants." We were ready to go.

During the drive I found myself continually amazed at the

78

easy beauty of California. In Washington the beauty is there also, hard-bought by months of cold and fog and rain. But California has been touched by an angel's wing.

The park had picnic tables, barbecue pits, ping-pong tables, tennis courts, a wonderful play area for little ones, a beautiful green which could be used for football, baseball, or even supposed golf. It was late fall, actually a beautiful time for a picnic, but the grounds were nearly deserted.

When we arrived, the boys unpacked the cars. We took two long brown tables with wooden benches for seats. Everything was soon settled. My table with our little Teresa, Joan, Germaine, and Jean was like a command post; from it, I could watch the family fan out in all directions.

Frank and the boys were playing football. It was actually a kicking contest. Frank, Nicky, and Tommy were on one side, Mike, Rusty, and Greg on the other. The idea of the game seemed to be that the two "teams" stood back and kicked the ball back and forth. If you kicked the ball over the heads of the other team, you got a point. The same was true if they didn't catch it. The little ones didn't have to catch the ball, only fall on it.

I had never seen Frank kick a football before and was surprised at his skill. Nicky and Tommy were wild with joy when Rusty dropped a kick. I guess an athlete never loses his style, because Frank covered almost every kick the boys made. Greg, of course, could not take the game seriously. He had to try drop kicking, place kicking, an on-side kick (which Tommy promptly fell on, to Frank's delight). But the punting contest between Frank, Mike, and Rusty continued. Urged on enthusiastically by Nicky, Tommy, Phillip, and little Gerry, Frank was punting deeper and deeper, pushing the bigger boys back to the edge of the forest.

I sat with the little children and watched the flow of the play. The young girls, Louise, Jean, Mary, Veronica, and Susan, were playing on the swings. Rosemary, Colleen, and Janette were mountain climbing in the hills. On the table before me was the huge lunch.

The football match ended as Frank kicked the ball far over the awed heads of his oldest sons and into the forest beyond. Manfully, all the men in the family plowed through the underbrush to look for the lost football, without success.

I called the girls and they ran to get the climbers. The men returned, Greg pretending to seriously dispute Tommy's contention that his side won. Greg was saying, "The side that loses the ball is penalized ten points. You were ahead by nine, so we win by one."

Tommy and Nicky both began sputtering objections, and Greg laughed. "I'm sorry. Of course your side wins. We didn't have a chance with Dad in good form."

I was thinking: What a table! Everyone had taken his place. We were quite a group. Frank stood at the head of the table and said grace. I looked at all those bowed heads, said grace with them, and added a short prayer that the new baby would be born strong and well.

After grace, Frank told them we had a family announcement to make. He told them very simply that with the help of God, we would have a new baby in the summer.

I think we have the cheeringest children in the world. They all raised a cheer and the older girls kissed me. They were delighted, even the young ones, who didn't know why they were cheering. It was almost as if everyone had been waiting for some new adventure, some overture of closeness, of family fun, to begin. Now they had it. The young children began finding out from the older ones why they had cheered.

Mike, who was sitting next to me, said quietly, "This is pretty great, Mom, isn't it?"

I said it was.

Being older, Mike was conscious of the past criticism our family received from sections of the public. "You think people are going to know how great it is?" he said.

Little Phillip called out, "Will its name be North or Beardsley, Mommy?"

"Beardsley," one of the children answered.

"When will the stork deliver it?"

"Next July."

"What a lazy bird!"

Greg, forever besieged by his sisters to keep his room neat, gave them a sly dig. "I hope it's a girl. She'll help me clean my room."

Frank started the food moving. I fed Joan and Teresa. Rosemary and Colleen presented Frank with the sandwich prepared for him. He looked down at it, astonished by its size. Greg said, "Dad, that may be the lost football."

Frank insisted I help him with the sandwich and cut off a portion for me, the girls following every move he made. He took a bite, smiled, and said it was great. The girls were pleased. I took a bite. It *was* great.

The first shadows fell too soon. Frank, Greg, Nicky, and Tommy made a heroic attempt to find the football. Mike and Rusty helped me get the leftovers together. The girls, sensing that the end of the picnic was near, were running from game to game, from swings to slides to hills, crowding in a taste of each form of pleasure. We managed to have everyone accounted for and all items packed before night fell and we drove home.

We were in bed before midnight. Frank was restless. "Are you asleep?" he asked me.

"No, I'm too happy. Wasn't it wonderful how the children responded to our announcement?"

"It was. I enjoyed that picnic. Do we have any calamine lotion, do you think?"

"We may. Do you feel itchy? I think there's some from the time last year when the girls walked into some poison oak. Frank, you don't suppose—"

"I'm afraid so. I'm the original seagoing city boy. I probably tramped right through it looking for that lost football."

"You think all the boys will come down with it?"

"I'm afraid so. We charged those woods like Teddy Roosevelt at San Juan Hill. I'm sorry, Helen."

"Don't be foolish. It could happen to anyone. I think I'd better find the lotion for you and then check the boys."

Nicky and Tommy were asleep, dead tired. I looked at them in the half light of their room and sure enough, they were in for a first-class case of oak poisoning, but I thought they would probably sleep until morning. Mike and Rusty had been spared, but Greg sat mournfully at the edge of his bed. "Mother, I'm sure glad to see you. I caught the hives or some strange Oriental disease."

"Poison oak."

"Poison oak?"

"Your Daddy has it, too. You got it chasing the football."

"What about Mike and Rusty?"

"No sign of it."

"I was searching like an all-American. They must have goofed off."

"Or they are better woodsmen than you."

"If you knew how I felt, you wouldn't insult my Boy Scout training."

"Use some of this lotion. I'll have to take it back to your father."

I was thankful the girls had not chosen that clump of

woods in which to mountain climb. I went back upstairs to Frank.

"What's the report?"

"Tommy, Nicky, Greg, and yourself."

"The real pros are stricken," he said, laughing. "I was aiming that last punt for the very edge of the field. The wind carried it a bit further. Did I ever tell you that when I played for the University of San Francisco I had punting duels with Al Braga, who still holds the University record for punting?"

There is no feeling of hunger that resembles the craving for a particular food felt during pregnancy. It is sharp as no hunger pain, lasting as a bruise. Difficult to talk yourself out of, impossible to ignore, the craving at times seems to consume you. Now, listening to Frank talk about football, I felt the beginnings of such a craving. All the senses seem to take part. You can smell the desired food, hear it being served, your mouth waters as if with the first taste. Yet I was still not certain exactly what I wanted to eat. Frank went on enthusiastically.

"At that time pro football was nothing. So college football was pretty much of a dead end. Sure, it was a chance to get an education, but football was so serious and time-consuming that you just didn't have time for serious study."

Suddenly I knew what I craved. It was a submarine sandwich like the one the girls had baked for Frank. I could taste the portion I had eaten at the picnic. The flavors of the meats and cheeses, the taste of pickle, of dressings. It was a completely absurd craving. Such cravings should be confined to green gumdrops, apple pie, coffee ice cream, and other very ordinary foods. But to have a craving for a submarine sandwich, prepared by children from no known recipe, made from odds and ends of schoolday lunches—it could not happen.

Frank said, "I'm sorry to be talking about football. You must be dead. I'll turn out the lights."

An hour passed. I was startlingly awake. I could almost reconstruct that sandwich. I recalled every suggestion made by the girls except what might Rosemary or Colleen have added on their own. I tried to identify each taste sensation.

Frank said, "Are you awake?"

"Yes."

"Hope I haven't kept you awake tossing around."

"You didn't. I'm just not sleepy. Doctors say if you just lie down and relax, it is as good for your system as sleep."

82

"I doubt it. You're not worried about anything?"

"No, certainly not."

"That's good."

He rolled over and started to breathe more deeply. Suddenly it occurred to me that he would know what was in that sandwich. After all, he knew exactly what he ate and he had eaten almost all of the sandwich, I thought enviously. So suddenly I asked, "You know what was in it, don't you, Frank?"

There was a second of silence. Then his voice, dragged back from sleep, said, "Know what was in what?"

"The submarine sandwich."

"It was in Reynolds wrap." He gave a comfortable sigh, as if he had solved a great problem. I said, a bit overanxiously, "You know what was inside the sandwich?"

"Are you talking in your sleep?"

"No. I just wondered if you knew what was inside the sandwich the girls prepared special for you."

"That was nice of them. I don't really know. Tasted as if everything was in it. You tell me."

"I just wondered. I don't know exactly. I heard them making it, but I don't actually know how many slices of salami or bologna, or how many slices of each cheese, or how many long slices of pickle, or how many dashes of French dressing."

Frank was staring at me now. "Helen, what difference does it make at this time of the morning?"

"Of course it doesn't make any difference. It's really neither here nor there, is it?"

"Helen, you're not hungry, are you? I could go down and get you a sandwich."

"No, please don't. You couldn't actually make one without the girls."

"You mean that submarine sandwich?"

"Didn't you like it?"

"It was great, but it wasn't a sandwich. It was a raging conflict."

"Was it really?"

"Sure, you tasted it."

"I thought it was great. It had a certain new dimension in food for me. It was as if I had stumbled into a magic village and the leprechauns prepared me a meal and there it was."

"I probably didn't praise it enough. I was thinking of that lost football."

"I only had a taste of it."

Finally he caught on. "You mean you *want* one of those things?"

I nodded.

He laughed. "I'll put on a robe and go down and make one. They baked it, didn't they?"

"They had French rolls, salami, bologna, ham, French dressing, Russian dressing, cheese, pickles, onions, tomatoes. I don't know what else. Frank, this is completely silly. You can't cook a sandwich right now."

"Of course I can."

We went down to the kitchen. This was a serious business. I didn't want to keep Frank up, but I did have a craving and I had developed an unexpected dash of ruthlessness. Frank carefully reconstructed the children's masterpiece. He wrapped it in foil and put it in the oven. By the time it was baked, I was ravenously hungry. Frank took it from the oven and unwrapped it.

I asked, "Will you have some, Frank?"

He looked a bit awed. "No, you go right ahead."

"I'll bring it upstairs. Can I get you something?"

"No, thanks, honey."

The sandwich was almost as good as the one at the picnic. But not quite. There was some mysterious element missing. A hint of fragrance was not there. I wondered what we could possibly have missed. Frank, by now, was enjoying the whole incident.

"Helen, you have quite a figure for a woman with eight children."

"Having children does not ruin your figure," I said, downing the last bite.

"How about submarine sandwiches from now until summer?"

"I never craved such a monumental item in my whole life. But don't mention it again."

The next morning we were back in the regular routine. But there was one slight interruption in the smooth-working family group. I was taking each of the girls aside and carefully recording her contribution to that picnic concoction. I had just questioned Mary when Frank noticed the notebook, the serious conversation. He began smiling and shaking his head.

I said quietly, "Not a word out of you, Frank Beardsley. I

84

was just making sure of the recipe in the remote possibility that I might sometime want to serve—"

"Of course, Helen." He gave me a kiss. "I'm very happy about the new baby, submarine sandwiches and all."

XV

Except for the birth of the baby, I don't think there was another occasion all of us looked forward to so eagerly in that first winter of our happiness as our first Christmas together. And as the slow round of days suddenly seemed to change their pace and move swiftly into December, I sometimes had the feeling that the children enjoyed the preparations even more than Frank and I did.

With twenty people all trying to prepare for Christmas in their own way, you can be sure that the expectation of the holiday was built up early. At the end of November, Mike, Rusty, and Greg suddenly took jobs as bag boys in the supermarket, working weekends; Rosemary and Colleen made sure to schedule extra babysitting jobs—all, of course, in order to earn "present money." I hadn't suspected how much the older children would want to have a hand in preparing surprises and fun for their littler brothers and sisters. For weeks before the twenty-fifth you could invariably find secret gatherings going on all over the house. All types of spies and couriers were being sent into the ranks of the youngsters to find out diplomatically what they wanted. With all the conclaves going on and with one member of the family sometimes involved in as many as four of them, I wondered how they could possibly keep secrets from each other.

After a while one scene became routine. A few of the children would be involved in a discussion. Another child would wander over, only to be met with sudden silence. It generally took the interloper only a moment to realize what was going on. "Christmas?" he'd say. The group would nod and the wanderer would gracefully withdraw.

Frank and I felt that the children were in the best position to find out what each of them wanted, and so when it came to sending out spies, we organized our own network, which I'm sure rivaled that of the CIA. We naturally had to be careful about the number and price of items we bought, but by keeping the gifts modest we easily managed to make sure that each child got pretty close to what he wanted. True, we spent some of the following months paying for everything, but it was more than worth it. Most of the older children's gifts were in the form of clothes, but we wouldn't dare make the mistake of giving the youngsters such unappealing items.

For Frank and me gifts at Christmas take second place to the larger gift of Christmas itself, and we tried to make the children aware that this was the time of Christ's birth. And so even as the presents were gradually being stock-piled in every out-of-the-way place that could be found, we also observed the tradition of lighting an Advent candle on each of the four Advent Sundays—three candles white for divine innocence and the fourth one rose, to indicate that the promise is near to fulfillment. And to let the children know that this was indeed Christ's birthday, we decorated a cake for the Child Jesus—complete with candles, which the littlest ones got to blow out.

Even weeks before Christmas we all found ourselves launching now and then into the traditional carols. A lot of people seem to find "the same old ones" tiresome, but not this family. With a few of us to throw in some fancy harmony, and the others who supplied more volume than tune, we found those some of the most pleasurable moments of the holiday. The outside of the house got into the act, too. Lights were decked all over it, and among the hillside flowers a sleigh and reindeer was landed for our Santa-Claus believers.

As the twenty-fifth neared on our first Christmas, the activity in the house was stepped up. Susan and Veronica, not to be out-surprised by the older children, decided on a surprise of their own. Choosing their cast from our younger set, they planned their own production (and version) of Dickens' *A Christmas Carol*. The TV set in their playroom was strangely silent night after night as they rehearsed.

Each day, it seemed, a Railway Express or United Parcel truck would stop outside the house with a gift package from one or another of our relatives. This brought the children hurrying to learn who had sent the present. As they took it away to be stored they speculated among themselves as to what could possibly be in it, trying to tell from its size, shape, and weight. They were on their honor not to shake or squeeze.

Three days before Christmas the tree was brought into the living room and set up. It looked big enough for a park in a small town and was so tall that we had to cut off the topmost branches. We had spent the previous days shopping, and the night the tree went up Frank and I had just returned home with the station wagon full of presents—only one load among many. Nonetheless, we could not resist decorating the tree that night. Mike, Rusty, and Greg pitched in, along with the older girls. When we were done it looked magnificent, but only the most hardy among us lasted through to the putting-on of the tinsel. For the next two days the job of wrapping all the gifts and placing them under the tree occupied almost all the waking hours—and many of the sleeping ones. In a family the size of ours it required the use of all the odd hours in order to keep those who believed in Santa Claus assured that we had not replaced him. It was fun each morning to watch the eyes of the little ones widen as, impossibly, the pile of presents grew higher and wider, higher even than some of their heads, until it seemed that if one present were dislodged the living room would be the scene of a gay-colored avalanche of no mean proportions.

On the afternoon before Christmas, Nicky and Tommy were in the living room putting the final touches on the Christmas crib—a small replica of the scene of the Nativity. Nicky wanted to put a cow in the stable with the Baby Jesus and Tommy objected. Mary was called in to settle the argument. "The cow belongs in the stable," she announced.

Tommy objected. "How'd you like to be born in a stable with some old cow lookin' at you?"

"Jesus didn't care at all," Mary replied, undaunted. "He wanted to show us that where you're born doesn't matter, and what you have doesn't matter. It's what you're like inside that matters."

"So then nice clothes don't matter?" Tommy asked.

Mary said no.

Nicky, siding with his brother against this onslaught of feminine authority, said, "And toys don't matter?"

"No."

"O.K.," Tommy said, "then presents don't matter either, and so you don't want any, right?"

There was a pause. "Oh, leave your old cow out if you want to," Mary said archly.

I stopped listening as Nicky bawled once more, "But I want it in!"

I know of no other night of the year when it is so easy to get little children bathed and into bed as on Christmas Eve. Our older girls had made beautifully decorated red and green felt stockings for all of us (that year there were twenty) and before each child went to bed he hung his stocking above the mantel. Of course, there was a little talk of waiting up for Santa, but even as the anticipation of the next day was still casting its glow about them, sleep was dimming the light in their eyes. And that night, as each of the younger children dropped off, the older children—all those over eleven were eligible—went off to midnight Mass, a treat for them.

Later, when everyone was in bed, Frank and I went on wrapping gifts that were to be last-minute surprises, filling stockings, and putting the final touches on things. While we were out shopping Frank had gleefully bought up a load of what he termed "real bargains"—toys which you could assemble yourself. At three-thirty in the morning he was still assembling a mass of complicated geometric shapes that were strewn all over the floor. I asked him if he wanted me to help him. His murmured reply was something like, "E-4 is then slid under the projecting cover of R-3 . . ."

Hardly able to keep my eyes open, I asked him again.

"No, Helen, of course not. You go on to sleep. I'll be through here in a couple of minutes."

The next morning when Frank shook me awake there was a note of triumph in his voice as he said, "Well, I did it."

"What?"

"Got that thing assembled before the kids came down."

Fully dressed, he started to take off his shirt.

"Are you going to tell me," I said foggily, "you've been awake all night?"

"Yep."

"Oh, no," I groaned.

"I'll be O.K. A quick shower and I'll feel like a million. I'll take a nap a little later."

It was barely past dawn, but with their built-in alarms working to perfection the children were already moving around the house. Tired, I found myself still able to feel that jolt of excitement from knowing it was Christmas Day, looking forward to taking the youngsters to church. I almost expected to see snow outside the window and feel the floor cold under my feet, for although I have traveled around the world and seen Christmas in many different lands, I still have to adjust to the balmy and frequently warm weather that accompanies Christmas in California.

Downstairs, Rosemary already had Christmas carols playing on the stereo and when some of the youngsters weren't milling about the huge piles of presents—which would be opened when we returned from Mass—they were after Frank and me to please take them to church.

When we returned from Mass it was to a house in which everyone was occupied with the particular job he had been delegated to do. And on this day I was to be more director than doer, for the offers of help were almost more numerous than I had chores for the hands. The younger children were now all over the place, urging their older brothers and sisters on to greater speed in serving the special breakfast. And when the table was ready it was apparent that this was a breakfast unlike any other. Crisp, pressed white sheets covered our two huge breakfast tables, and they in turn had been decked with pine branches, cones, and sprigs of holly. Alongside of each plate was a chocolate Santa, and the table had also been decorated with a great Christmas centerpiece. Orange juice, the one and only concession to nutrition, was followed by hot brown cocoa with whipped cream, baked eggs in bologna cups, and all the buttered sweet rolls one could eat.

From breakfast on it became the children's day. And if children are easy to get to bed on Christmas Eve, they are a joy to watch on Christmas Day. I can't think of a time when they are kinder or more charitable, and their Ohs and Ahs, their Thank you, Daddys and Thank you, Mommys and the glow on their faces make it wonderful to be a parent to so many—erasing as if by magic the long hours of worry, care, and attention they've needed all year. I sometimes think that the New Year really starts at Christmas, when the joy of giving and receiving adds renewed vigor to everyone and revives our feeling of good will to all.

When we were all assembled around the tree Mike, Rusty, and Greg took turns giving out the presents and Frank and I sat back to enjoy the fruits of our labor. Rusty had argued for a baseball cap for Phillip, but Frank had disagreed with him, saying that baseball was out of season.

"Dad, I'm telling you, that's what he wants," Rusty had insisted.

Frank had bought it, but under protest. Now Phillip put the baseball cap on and smiled with pleasure. Ignoring his other presents, he tugged at the peak. "Gee, Daddy," he said, "just what I really wanted. How'd ya know?"

Frank look at Rusty, who was grinning from ear to ear. "Instinct, son," Frank said wryly. "Pure instinct."

Later in the day, after the mountains of gift wrappings had been cleared, the girls went about preparing dinner. We had spent the better part of two days on the menu and with all of the things that had to be done our house might well have been dubbed Beardsley's Restaurant. Two twenty-pound turkeys had been roasting for hours and were now ready for the table. Accompanying them would be four casserole dishes full of crisp salad, ten pounds of mashed potatoes with giblet gravy, four quarters of butter, forty fresh-baked rolls, four serving dishes of cranberry sauce, olives, pickles, stuffed celery, vegetables, sweet potatoes, pitchers of chilled cider, and even wine for Frank and me.

Setting and decorating the massive table was a major task, but for the willing hands that did the job it was fun that came too rarely. Out came the linen, handmade in Hong Kong, and as the girls went to it the table gradually began to gleam with over a hundred pieces of sterling silver, candelabra, and stemware.

During the last-minute preparations Colleen came over to me. "Mommy, you're going to have to do something about Phillip. I can't get him out of the kitchen."

"What's the matter?"

"He keeps watching the turkeys through the oven window and says that he's gotta have a drumstick."

I took Phillip aside and asked him why he was bothering his sisters.

"I didn't mean to," he said. "I just wanted to see how the turkeys cook."

"Is that all?"

He shook his head. "I was wondering, too."

"About what?"

"About who gets a drumstick."

"Did you want one?"

"Yes."

"But the drumstick is dark meat, Phillip, and you don't like dark meat."

90

"Oh, but I really do when it's a drumstick," he answered. In another minute I found out what the problem was. A little friend of his, it seemed, had asked Phillip if he ever got a drumstick. Phillip said no, and his friend said that Phillip never would, because all his older brothers and sisters probably grabbed them first. "He said I'll probably never get one till I'm old," Phillip ended gloomily, forgetting he had never wanted one.

Just before we went in to dinner I had a chance to ask Frank about Phillip's problem. He looked puzzled for a moment. Then he said, "Does he know how big those drumsticks are?"

"I guess he does."

The girls called us to the table, and as all of the family gathered around it there were murmurs of awe from the children. Tall tapers had been placed at each end, and beside each plate was a large gumdrop with a birthday candle in its center and a Lifesaver pushed into its side for a handle. The candles were lit, casting their soft light over everything. "We can't eat that," Rusty said, almost involuntarily. "It's too beautiful." In complete agreement our nineteen ladies and gentlemen sat down. But after grace had been said and the food was served, they soon rediscovered their appetites.

As Frank started to carve the first turkey, he paused. "I've had a serious question placed before me by Master Phillip . . . Would you like to ask the question yourself, Phillip?"

The little boy nodded solemnly. "Yes. Who gets the drumstick?"

"I'd say, Phillip, that everyone who really wants the drumstick should get one, wouldn't you?"

Phillip nodded.

"Then my ruling is that we all share it. In this family, we all get the drumstick."

Phillip indicated his younger brother. "Gerry, too?"

"Gerry, too. What do you think of that?"

"I think that's pretty good."

The rest of the children cheered and the meal was begun, ending only after four quarts of ice cream had been brought in, along with two cakes and three pumpkin pies.

The day would not have been complete, of course, without a show, provided in this case by the Beardsley Home Theater Players, none of whom exceeded the age of twelve. What their production of *A Christmas Carol* lacked in polish it made up for in purpose. Nicky appeared as Scrooge, wearing an old uniform of Frank's, and not even the fact that his pants kept falling down in the high dramatic moments distracted us from the seriousness of the drama.

And so the beautiful day passed, spiced occasionally with the friendliness of neighbors who dropped in to wish us well. When it was over Frank and I were almost asleep on our feet.

"I think we should start getting ready," Frank said.

"What for?"

"Next year. I'm worn out."

I laughed. "It was worth it, though, wasn't it?"

"It was worth it," Frank said quietly. "Every moment of it."

XVI

As with everything one spends a lot of time preparing for, Christmas seemed too soon over. New Year's Eve and Day sped swiftly by also, and then California's winter came in, so gently one hardly seemed to realize it was there: months of some slight rain that deepened the green in the trees of Carmel; a season of problems and their adjustment; a season of deepening understanding and love between Frank and myself and among all of our children. By spring Michael and Rusty were going to their first formals. They were impressive young gentlemen, dressed in their tuxes, quite startling because the ordinary California attire is so casual, different from that of a formal date. And that spring, Rosemary had her first date with a boy from the high school and I had to spend quite a bit of time coaching Mike, Rusty, Greg, and Frank into not appearing too hearty, too folksy, too interested, too surprised, when the boy arrived to take Rosemary out.

Soon spring, too, was gone. Underlying most of our other concerns now was the anticipation of the new baby, due sometime in the first part of July. With vacations on, the character of the house changed. There was still the quiet time at night when everyone had gone to bed, but we didn't have that beautiful pause somewhere around eight-thirty in the morning when the people going to school had left the house.

We had the natural anxieties any parents have before childbirth, but everything seemed to be going well. Spring had moved suddenly into summer, as it does in this part of California, and there was very little change in our situation.

Then, one night in early July, I lay awake hour after hour with recurring pains. I hated the idea of a false alarm. It was almost an obsession with me not to go to the hospital too early. So I didn't wake Frank right away. I lay in bed and tried to time the contractions, quite certain that I was at least two weeks away from having this baby. Then suddenly, about three-thirty, I was equally certain I had waited too long. I shook Frank.

He awoke slowly. I said, "Frank, get up and get everything ready, you have to take me to the hospital."

I lay very still, not daring to move, while Frank dressed quickly and began to pack some things for me. At one point he stopped and looked at me with a puzzled expression. "If this is so urgent," he said, "why don't you get up?"

"I'll explain later. Please hurry, Frank." A couple of minutes later, while he was in the bathroom, I felt I could make it to the station wagon safely. Getting up, I wrapped the blanket around me, gingerly walked downstairs, and made my way to the carport. With a sigh of relief, I stretched myself out on the back seat of the station wagon and lay there waiting for Frank. I waited for what seemed hours. Finally I heard him in the kitchen. A moment later he poked his head out the kitchen door, peered at the car, then ran back in the house.

In exasperation, I called out loud enough to wake the neighborhood.

"Helen?" he yelled back from somewhere in the house.

"Frank, will you hurry up?"

There was panic in the voice that answered. "Where are you?"

"In the car!"

What I didn't know, of course, was that when Frank had come out of the bathroom and seen I was gone, he went looking all over the house for me. When he'd popped his head out the kitchen door he failed to see me, since I was lying down. Needless to say, by the time he found me both of us were frantic.

Frank gently took the car down our steep incline to the

road below. To make things worse, an unusually heavy early morning fog shrouded the road, forcing Frank to drive very slowly.

Impatiently, I said, "Frank, you've got to go faster."

"I can't," he said. After a few moments he added, "I think the only thing we can do is stop at the Navy Air Facility and get an ambulance."

When we arrived there, Frank got out of the car and went inside. A few moments later I was startled by a young corpsman who had materialized out of the fog and was gazing down at me. If I had not felt so panicky I know I would have laughed at his question. It sounded straight from the manual.

"Is this your first pregnancy, ma'm?" he asked guilelessly.

"No," I said, teeth clenched.

"That's fine, ma'm. How far apart are your contractions?"

I said sharply, "Have you ever delivered a baby?"

"No, ma'm."

"Then you'd better get an ambulance here fast or you'll be delivering your first and my ninth child right on this seat."

The young corpsman's eyes widened and he dashed off into the building.

I was somewhat relieved a few moments later as the ambulance approached. Friendly and capable hands assisted me into it and helped me onto the stretcher inside.

"You'd better follow in the car," a voice said to Frank. "If the baby comes you'd only be in the way."

As the rear door slammed I caught a glimpse of Frank. Standing there, fog-shrouded, he had an air of desolation about him. At first I thought I imagined it, but as the ambulance rumbled on the expression on his face kept returning to me. I had never seen him look so sad. I wondered if it had been something I said, and I wished that he were with me so that I could assure him I would be all right. I had an image of him following the ambulance, worried and alone, as we sped to Fort Ord. And then suddenly, in a rush of shame that I hadn't realized it before, the reason why he looked so forlorn came to me.

This was the very same journey, made with the same sense of emergency, that Frank had taken in the ambulance which took his wife, Frances, to her death.

I wished now that I had not acted so impatient with him. When you are deeply in love with someone there is a sixth sense that instinctively lets you know what he is thinking. I knew somehow that Frank must now be comparing the same fog-draped highway, the strange circumstance that had him driving again over the same road that had meant such tragedy for him before. True, this time the journey was to bring a new life to his family, but that other memory was still there.

When the ambulance reached the hospital at Ford Ord I had only a second to squeeze Frank's hand and tell him I was fine before an attendant gave him some forms and told him to fill them out. The doctor looked at me closely, then looked again, and then said to Frank, "When you come back after you fill out those forms I'll tell you whether it's a boy or a girl."

Twenty minutes later Joseph John Beardsley was born.

It was 5:42 in the morning. I hadn't been in the hospital long enough to have any anesthesia and I looked at this new born life and thought: How can anyone alive not revere life? To see the beauty of a newborn child is more startling than the most glorious southern sunset; more enchanting than purple mists on the mountains. What could be more beautiful than a new little life? A little form born of love? What sounds could quicken your heart, what knowledge fall more happily to your mind than the recognition of a new little life? So this little man, Joseph John Beardsley, impressed me mightily. He looked from that first minute exactly like Frank himself must have looked as a baby—a chubby body with a pink complexion. He was exactly what people mean when they talk of a spanking baby boy.

At night in the hospital I lay awake and thought of Joseph John and the children at home. I was very anxious to be home with them. I couldn't wait to bring the baby to them. By now I thought of all of them collectively—the family. I never thought of them as two families. In my mind the two families had merged totally, and the birth of Joseph John would bring the children even closer than they were.

But the new baby was important for more than this. He was a blessing over the new love between Frank and me. He was our answer to the weak-hearted, those afraid of life; more, he was our answer to our own fears. We placed little Joseph John Beardsley and his future into the hands of the Lord with faith that was a reflection of Abraham's. By all the rules of our time and society we should have been afraid. We had by any modern standards too many children to support and raise properly. Now we had another. Joseph John Beardsley was the greatest act of faith we could perform. I hugged him as a mother and loved the life in him and was deeply grateful that his father was a man of faith in an age of doubt.

I had seen Frank just briefly after the baby was born, before the doctor gave me a sedative so that I might sleep. We were both too overcome to say anything, so he had just pressed my hand. When he visited me later, though, he was as excited as a boy might be, his eyes shining, his face flushed with excitement.

"He's a beautiful, beautiful baby."

"He looks like his father."

"I don't know about that, but he is rather a handsome fellow."

"How did the children take it?"

"They couldn't be happier. They are very, very excited. The older ones are delighted for us. The little ones can't wait for us to bring their baby brother home."

"I'm very happy, Frank."

"So am I. It's strange, but I sat outside in that car this morning and wondered at the way things happen. There I was sitting in the very same corridor on the very same bench where just a couple of years ago I had sat while the doctors tried to save Frances' life. Now I was here and a new life was being born. I was acutely aware of the providence of God, and its role in our love."

We were both quiet for a moment, then Frank gave me a hug and went down the hall to get another look at Joseph John. He came back all smiles. He said to me with great enthusiasm, "That fellow deserves a good launching. We'll have a family party after his christening."

I had to smile because it was this quality of sudden enthusiasm which made Frank appear so young. I was quick to go along with him. So while I was in the hospital, I made the plans for a family party to celebrate the baby's baptism.

Frank visited me often and told me how the children were getting along. Day by day, he said, they were building up to the arrival of their new brother. Frank told me that the girls were vying with each other for the honor of taking care of this young man and I knew that we would have to spread this duty very fairly so no one would feel left out of it.

We went home after a few days. The children were waiting for us on the hill as Frank drove up to the house. Greg and Mike had put up a huge sign across the carport—WELCOME HOME JOSEPH JOHN. The girls had decorated the house as if

96

for a party. The whole mood of the family was one of excitement and pure joy. I think without being able to put it into words, probably without realizing it consciously, the children felt the way Frank and I did—that the baby represented a greater bond between the two families, the one who belonged to all of us. They didn't have to say it; their actions showed it.

XVII

Joseph John was baptized at the Carmel Mission at which Frank and I had been married, on a beautiful summer day. The sky was breathtakingly blue; green hills led to the glittering blue sea. It was a perfect day. Two of Frank's sisters, Sister Mary Eleanor and Sister Mary Anselm, received permission to come to the house. His brother Vincent and his wife Aileen came to be the godparents, those who were to be "spiritual" parents for Joseph John if anything happened to us. Other members of both families came too, and with our children, it could not fail to be a lively party.

When Frank proudly showed Aileen and Vincent the baby, Aileen said, "Isn't he beautiful, Vin?"

Vin knitted his brow. "I'm not sure," he said. "He looks to me like Frank shrank."

The occasion was made even happier for us all by the fact that after two families had been touched by tragedy and gone through a long, tough period, they were now in a position to celebrate the advent of new life.

The house was alive with excitement. As our families arrived, the children seemed to absorb their uncles and aunts easily, taking them off to show them their rooms, talking with them. And the grownups were intrigued. It probably brought them back to memories of the day when all families were nearly as large as this one.

I joked with Sister Mary Eleanor, accusing her of setting all this in motion. Her wise eyes took in the children, the house, and her brother Frank with obvious delight.

97

Of course the high point of the day was the actual ceremony of the Sacrament of Baptism, signifying to us that the stain of the original sin with which man was born had been removed, and that this little boy was a child of God and an heir of Heaven. It was a touching ceremony which meant to me that he was now spiritually alive, he had become a member of the Christian community. He was joining the faithful on earth, that group of baptized Christians throughout the whole world, and he now truly had a brothership with man. This was the union of which John Donne was speaking when he said:

When the Church baptizes a child, that action concerns me; for that child is thereby connected to that body which is my head too and engrafted into that body whereof I am a member. All mankind is of one author and is one volume . . . No man is an island entire of itself. Every man is a piece of the continent, a part of the main. If a clod be washed away by the sea, Europe is the less. Any man's death diminishes me, because I am involved in mankind. And therefore never send to know for whom the bell tolls; it tolls for thee.

That was the high point of the day for me, the realization that little Joseph John had now joined this great community of mankind.

I enjoyed all the visitors. I enjoyed seeing people who had been so kind to me on a sadder occasion. And there was a lot of pride and joy for me in showing these children how well we had all survived under the providence of the Almighty.

It was only when finally the house settled down and I was dropping off to sleep quite exhausted that I suddenly felt I had something important to tell Frank. I was too tired to remember exactly what it was. Then I remembered. I touched Frank's shoulder. He stirred sleepily.

"Frank?" I said, almost asleep myself. "I remembered something important to tell you."

"What is it?"

His voice was that of a man who had greeted too many relatives, relived too many memories, and had too long a day.

I said dreamily, "Joseph John Beardsley is a child of God and an heir of Heaven."

"That's nice," I heard him say. And then I was asleep.

XVIII

Summer had gone. The children were back in school. This time I had planned the shopping for their school outfits carefully. I would never again become involved in a shopping experience like the one I had the previous fall. With the school-age children gone most of the day and only the little ones around, the days went by in peaceful routine.

Time had eased any awkwardness in the relationships among the children. They had formed their natural affinities, which seemed to be a part of life in a large family. They knew what we expected and they knew exactly what they could do and what they could not do. It was quite an ordered existence. Yet I don't think it was in any way harsh.

We never quite got beyond the stage of living on a close budget. I had to buy food very carefully, almost by lots, at sale time in order to keep the food budget within limits. It meant a good deal of chicken, which we could buy cheaply and freeze; it meant a lot of variations on hamburgers and meat loaves; and yet we survived rather well.

Of course, we had decisions that had to be made. We had to consider what Michael's career might be. Rosemary had to have an eye operation which, while it was not serious, was extremely delicate. And I frankly prayed that we would avoid any major illness. For even a summer cold quickly became an epidemic; and a siege with the flu was exactly that—a siege —because it spread from one to another and soon there were perhaps a dozen very miserable children to take care of.

But life had its light side, too. Frank and I had had to formulate a strict family policy on pets. It was a difficult decision to make, but we simply couldn't allow animals for the children. If we did we might easily have ended up with our own private zoo.

The girls were in love with horses; the boys to a man wanted dogs; and, of course, the little girls loved kittens. When any of our children questioned the rule by pointing out that other families had pets, I admitted to them that they were right. I pointed out to them, however, that our children were compensated for this by having more built-in playmates than any other family. I was afraid to make one exception lest I open the door to eighteen more.

To all appeals for special pets, Frank and I had to present a united and sometimes stern front. We have persuasive, very, very charming children, so that frequently we have to offer a stern façade to them despite the fact that we'd like nothing better than to give in to their wishes and surrender to their charm, if only to watch the expressions on their faces.

My worry is not that I may not have enough time for each child, but that one of them may enchant me into spending too much time with him.

The children tested us on the no-pet rule just as often as they did on any other. Phillip had now become the leader of the little ones, and he brought the problem up at dinner.

"Daddy, if a giant pet, a gorilla, followed us home, could we keep him?"

Frank considered the question gravely. "A gorilla?"

The little ones nodded in unison.

"I think he would be classified as a pet and you'd have to get rid of him."

Phillip persisted. "But suppose he was a *big* gorilla and he was in my room, I mean in Gerry's and my room. Suppose he was so big we *couldn't* put him out."

"I don't care how big he is. You brought him in. You'd be responsible for getting him out."

"A big dog, too?"

Frank nodded and the question was settled. We were discreet enough to stay away from Gerry and Phillip's room until after all the panting and tugging and grunting was over and their "gorilla" was removed.

The older boys tested the rule in a different way. Nicky and Tommy had become nature enthusiasts. They loved to hike in the hills surrounding Carmel Bay and bring home interesting stones, shells, and pieces of wood. One day they found what they called a "horny toad." They had carried the toad home and built a little box-home for it on the hill outside the house. One night at dinner they presented their problem.

"Dad, would an 'outside' horny toad be considered a pet?"

Frank pondered. In truth, Frank is a city man and I wasn't certain if he knew exactly what a "horny toad" was. But I

think the "outside" part appealed to him. He asked Nick,
"You mean this toad is kept outside?"

"Yes, sir, in a little box we built."

"Then it lives in its own house."

"Tommy and I built it."

"Will we have to buy food for it?"

"No, sir."

"In that case I think the horny toad would not be classified as a pet."

There were broad smiles around the table. They included mine. Maybe he had bent the rule a bit but I agreed with him. The boys later added an "outside" lizard they found. What none of us realized was that Frank's judgment in this minor case was to set a precedent in the case of Cindy, the cocker spaniel.

A gentle and beautiful black cocker who belongs to a neighbor, Cindy visited our house one morning and found the Beardsley little ones playing a game that interested her. She joined in the fun for a while and then she dutifully returned to her owners.

The next morning she was back again, a little earlier than the previous one. The visits soon became a habit. Each morning she arrived earlier and earlier at our house, waited for Phillip, Germaine, Gerry, and Joan, and joined whatever game they were playing. She was quite a charming dog, a bit whimsical as she followed the little ones in a procession in front of our house, stopping occasionally to watch a black-winged butterfly or something else that interested her, then hurried to join the children. The dog almost seemed to know of the no-pet rule, observing a self-imposed curfew which kept her out of Frank's sight. It wasn't long before Frank became aware of Cindy, however, and one night at dinner, Frank brought the problem before the family. "I think I have observed a black dog about our home. Could this be possible?"

Phillip's eyes were big. "That's Cindy."

"A very nice name, but—"

"But she's not our dog."

Frank asked in mock severity, "Then why do I find her asleep in our carport at dawn? Why do I find her parading proudly outside my picture window at dusk?"

Susan said, "Daddy, Cindy is a special dog. She isn't ours. She just comes over and plays with the children."

Teresa said brightly, "She has floppy ears."

101

Frank measured his words. "You mean the dog who almost lives with us or who lives with us all my waking hours is not ours? How can that be?"

Now he faced a solid front. "She's not ours," they chorused.

Mary, who along with all the other older children was completely enjoying the scene, said, "Dad, she's from next door. She just likes to play with the Beardsleys."

Frank surveyed the roomful of dancing eyes. "Am I to believe this dog has chosen us?"

"Yes," the children said.

"Then are we not legally responsible for her snaps or her bites? And since she spends almost as many hours here as a member of the family, is she not clearly a pet under the family rule against pets?"

There was a chorus of noes. Frank pretended to be dismayed. The older children were amused. The youngsters were jumping with enthusiasm over the idea of Cindy legally evading the rule.

"You see, Dad," Rusty said. "Cindy comes under the same ruling you made for the toad and the lizard. She's got her own house and we don't buy food for her."

There was a long pause, then Frank said solemnly, "I think that the dog, Cindy, not being owned by a member of this family, and having of her own desire and with permission of her owners elected to spend certain hours with certain Beardsleys, this same dog should be considered an 'outside' dog and is therefore not subject to the family no-pet rule. Case dismissed."

Later that night, when the children were asleep and Frank was dozing off, I couldn't resist teasing him.

"You didn't leave much of that rule. I suppose if a horse wanders up here and stays days, we are stuck with another exception."

Frank said sleepily, "I don't think a horse will . . . That dog is pretty cute. What does she do, play with the little ones all day?"

"She actually protects them. Once when the gas man came, Cindy raised Cain until I came out."

"That's good."

"What about the rule? First 'outside' horned toads, then lizards, then a dog who visits. What else?"

He opened one eye and looked at me. "I draw the line at Phillip's gorilla."

Then he was asleep.

XIX

It was some time before I realized that several of the younger children were having a problem at grade school. At the Mission School they all attended you could find Beardsleys all the way from the first to the eighth grade. The first time the problem came up was one evening when Susan was helping Nicky with his homework, but at the time I was busy with something and their conversation didn't register with me. Nicky had apparently written the name North at the top of his paper.

"How come you write Nicholas *North?*" Susan said. "It should be Beardsley."

"Sister won't let me."

"But you're my brother and *I'm* Beardsley."

"I wanted to write it." He struggled for a moment to remember exactly what his teacher had told him. "But Sister said I'm not a *legal* Beardsley so I can't."

I remembered the conversation a few weeks later when Tommy approached me in that subtle, roundabout way that children have of discussing important things with adults.

"Are we one family or not, Mom?"

"Of course we're one family."

"Joey Martin says we're not one family at all. He says we're two families."

"He can say what he pleases; you all have the same mother and father, right?"

"That's what I said. Do you know what he said?"

"Something foolish, I imagine."

"He said we have different names, we don't sit together in school, and we're not truly brothers and sisters like he and his family."

"You may as well get used to your friends saying this and that about you. You'll find one or two boys like that anywhere."

"It's not just Joey. Billy Harkins said it and he's one of my best friends."

"Maybe some of your friends are jealous just because you belong to such a large family."

"Mom, it's not just *my* friends. They say it to Mary, Colleen, Janette, and Nicky."

"I'll talk to your daddy about it. Then we'll talk again."

Children, I thought—what a strange world it is in which they live. No doubt all the talk about the marriage and the new baby had caused some of the children in school to resent our children. It was perfectly natural, but I didn't want them to be hurt. It brought me to a problem Frank and I had once before put off acting on: the legal adoption of the children. This would mean that I would adopt the Beardsley children and Frank would adopt the Norths. All the children would then have the same name. Thus if anything happened to Frank or myself the survivor would have the legal control of all the children. We wanted these children to suffer no more separations and upsets, but we had purposely delayed legal proceedings.

Months before Joseph John's birth, Frank had contacted John Hopkins, a San Francisco attorney friend of his father's. John, because he was so enthusiastic about our marriage and felt that the adoption was imperative, had offered to handle the adoptions without a fee. The usual cost of $250 per child, if held to, would actually have forced us to abandon the idea. Although John wanted to begin the preliminary work on the adoptions, we had held back from making the final decision to go into court. We had already experienced the kind of attention such a move would bring to us when a story of our marriage in a national magazine had mistakenly mentioned that we had adopted each other's children. The reaction was frightening. Letters condemning us for being heartless arrived from all over the country. Some were intentionally cruel, written purposely to wound. But the type of letter that hurt to the point of tears was written by people whose criticism was genteel in mood but nonetheless full of recrimination. Here is one which was addressed to me personally.

Dear Mrs. Beardsley:

When I read of your marriage, my reaction was one of immeasurable sadness for your deceased husband. Silenced by death, how would he feel knowing his children had been robbed of his name? He must have been so proud of each child, proud of each child bearing his name, knowing the "North" name would be carried on.

Of course, it's more convenient for you and your new husband this way. But to wipe out a man's name from his child is to destroy his memory. It looks as if you couldn't wait to wipe out the last trace of his ever having existed.

Think it over. I was widowed too but I never robbed my son of his father's name.

Sincerely,

It was not the vituperative, crank-style letter. It was calm and even advisory. It cut to the heart.

Such reactions had been partially responsible for causing us to delay the adoptions, but something that affected us even more than this was the attitude of Dick's older brother, Bill. He had heard through the family grapevine that we were contemplating adoption. He and his family paid us a surprise visit. When the subject came up, Bill was vehement in his objections. Were he himself to die, he said, he would have no objection to his wife's remarrying, but under no circumstances would he want his children to carry someone else's name. Because he respected Frank and me, he said, he respected our decision—but he would never agree with it. He cautioned us to consider how Dick would feel about his name being taken away. "And then ask yourselves if you're doing the right thing by him," he concluded.

It was this last point added to everything else which affected us—Frank even more than me—and stopped us from going forward with the adoption. We discussed the problem for countless hours, but each time we ended up in the same place. As a man, particularly as a Navy man, Frank seemed compelled to repeat the question Bill had posed. Our discussions always seemed to end with: "Are we being fair to Dick?"

"I don't know," I would answer.

"Neither do I," Frank would say tiredly.

Dick's mother wrote to us to say that she had heard about Bill's reaction. She urged us not to let it influence us, saying that as weighty a matter as this was our concern alone and that we must do what we felt was best. Still we could not bring ourselves to go ahead.

"I can't do it, Helen," Frank said, "I can't just shrug it off and say, 'Well, I know Dick would want us to do what we thought was right.' It's not enough."

105

And so we had delayed. Knowing in our hearts that it was the right and necessary thing to do, we delayed. But now, with the children continuing to bring up the subject of their names and the difficulties at school, the problem had to be faced squarely.

In our room, after the children were asleep, Frank and I talked well into the night. Once more we went over the same ground we had covered before, but this time we could not shy away from the fact that a decision had to be made. And as the hours passed it became obvious to us what the decision had to be. The important thing to these children was to be part of a unit. Everything they did showed it. Even before our wedding, when they knew we were going to be married, the children had started to call us Mommy and Daddy. Children are not concerned with judicial matters, they are concerned with being wanted, and each of our children—especially when our new family was first formed—wanted desperately to be just as much a part of it as the next one. Their reasoning was that I had changed *my* name; why couldn't they? So that from the day of the wedding each of the Norths had started to call himself Beardsley. "Now we're all a family," one would say. "We're all Beardsleys," said another. This was why they chose to put their new name on school papers and were disturbed when some of the teachers insisted that they put North, since Beardsley was not legal for them.

I loved the father of those children dearly, with a kind of love they themselves were too young to know. I will never forget him, just as I know that Frank will never forget his Frances. Having known Dick, I know that he would not want to jeopardize the happiness of his children. He would not have wanted anything to stand in the way of their security, emotionally or financially.

I had learned after Dick's death that he had very carefully prepared in advance for possible tragedy. Due to his foresight I had no legal or financial problems to contend with. It was this same type of foresight which had led Frank and me, even before we were married, to discuss the necessity of adopting each other's children. Besides the fact that it would make us all one family legally, it is the only sane procedure in such a case. By adoption each child becomes an equal partner in any family estate. I understood this and so did Frank.

How could Frank and I believe, therefore, that Dick or

Frances would be a party to denying the children anything that would make their lives here on earth more secure emotionally and materially? Dick and Frances have reached, we believe, their goal of eternal happiness. Who knows but that the greater feeling of oneness that their children will achieve, the true feeling of belonging and being wanted to the ultimate degree, will make it easier for one or more of them to reach that goal himself? This life of ours has enough obstacles.

Frank and I will see to it that each of these children knows and admires his parentage. These were good and wonderful people, and their memories will always be cherished; but it is not so much that Dick and Frances have a right to be known to the children as that the children have the right to know who and what *they* are. We have all the children's birth certificates and will see that some day each child is given his own. We have picture albums from both sides of the family and the children have been through them from time to time —interestingly enough, without sadness or tears. And why? Not because they loved their parents less but because children live for today and tomorrow and they love us, the living, and we love them. We only become silly enough to live in the past after we should be old enough to know better.

Near the end of our discussion, Joseph John woke up and began to toss around in his crib. Frank went over to him and started to play with him, making funny faces and sounds. But his mind, I knew, was on what we were talking about. Has anyone written that our babies can renew us when we are exhausted by the complications of adult life?

I stared out at the darkened landscape, the hills that led to the sea. Finally Frank broke the silence.

"Well, we're certainly not protecting the children by putting it off, are we?" Joseph John had curled a tiny fist around Frank's index finger and was tugging at it. Frank tugged back gently. "And that's our job—to protect them."

Joseph John gurgled and I said, "You see, he's quite untouched by all this talk. He's already settled. No one has to adopt him."

Frank's face brightened as he continued the miniature tug-of-war. I actually think he thought that Joseph John was a miracle of some kind. I had always heard old-wives' tales that children born at the end of a family were intelligent and lucky. And this fellow was already a strong personality in the house.

"There's something very important you're going to have to do, Helen."

"What's that?"

"Have a serious discussion with Colleen, Janette, and the rest. I'd like them to know what we are going to do, and why."

"I thought we could talk about it with them together."

"I'd rather you did it. If they have any questions they'd be more likely to bring them up with me absent. I want to be sure that as much as they can, they understand, so the decision will be totally their own."

I agreed.

I no longer held family conferences of only the Norths. We tried to discourage any splitting-off of the families, however slight. But I had a chance to talk to Colleen, Janette, Nicky, and Tommy.

I talked to the girls while I was feeding Joseph John. They were changing his crib. All the children had wanted to be assigned to take care of him. I was afraid they would spoil him outrageously. He was a little man of such good-natured placidity that he was hard for anyone to resist. I said, "Tommy told me some of the boys at school were bothering him because he's not really a Beardsley."

Colleen said briskly in her little-mother manner, "That's how fourth-graders are, Mother."

I had had a teacher in fourth grade who used to say there was a Chinese proverb: "The stones in the street cry out against the cruelty of fourth-graders."

I smiled. "You mean no one else has heard remarks?"

Janette said solemnly, "Nothing important. Anyone," she said, coming over and holding one pink toe of Joseph John, "I mean, no one can say he isn't our real brother."

"Do some of the children say you're not all one family?"

"Just some jealous ones. We really don't mind."

"Suppose we went to court and asked the judge to legally declare you all to be brothers and sisters. What would you think of that?"

"The kids at school still wouldn't believe it."

"They would if the judge at the same time gave you all the same family name."

Janette asked, "Which name would he give us, North or Beardsley?"

Colleen said quickly, "Beardsley. The family always takes

the name of the father. Just like when you get married; you take your husband's name."

Janette smiled. "That was a silly question."

I could see she was trying the name for size in her mind: Janette Deen Beardsley. She was sure and quick as she made the bed, and I watched her with pleasure. Now she was a poised, confident little girl, when only a short time before she had been grief-shattered. I wondered how she had endured it all so well. It was something else I owed to Frank, this confidence and care he had rekindled in Janette's mind.

Colleen asked interestedly, "What do you have to do, Mother, just go into court and tell them we want our names changed?"

"No, there's more to it than that. It's a complicated process to decide legally if your father can give you a proper home, and if he's a proper parent."

"Gee, we could tell them that. This house has more rooms than any others around here. And Daddy is great; we can tell the judge that."

"Don't get all worked up about it; we haven't finally decided to do it yet. What do you think the boys would think of the idea?"

Colleen dismissed the boys with a very young lady's impatience.

"They'll be all for it. It would make them more like Mike, Rusty, and Greg."

She was right. Mike with his unfailing kindness, Rusty with his knack for handling younger boys, and Greg with his good humor had become the idols of Nick and Tom.

My boys had changed. Nicky, who had formerly been a poor student, was now earning straight B's. And it was not only the boys who had changed all the way down the line my children had changed for the better since my marriage to Frank. Colleen, too, had been doing poor work in school, but competition with Louise had upped her grades. Janette and Frank's Mary had accomplished wonders of improvement in their school work by helping each other. Their personalities were different, too; they were more sure of themselves. And when had little Phillip stopped hanging on my apron strings, I wondered? Before my marriage he was always upset when I left the house to go somewhere. Now he had become independent—especially of me. It was not so long ago, it seemed, to me, when I had worried about the boys, wondered how they would grow up. Now they had these debonair high school brothers to imitate. They would not object to having a family name in common with Mike, Rusty, and Greg. And they told me this very quickly.

The children's reaction heartened me, and I knew that Frank and I were doing the right thing—that it was the only thing for us to do. For if anything should happen to me I would not want anyone but him to bring up these children. I didn't know another person alive who would attempt it or who could possibly do it but Frank.

The human heart has a staggering capacity for love. I was certain once that every part of my being was filled with the love of my children. Then I fell in love with Frank. My feelings for my children were not in the slightest way diminished in my heart; rather, my love for them was enriched as I came to know Frank's children. But how could I say this to Bill?

That same night, when I told Frank what the children had said, he beamed. "Helen, I think we've got just about the finest family in the world . . . What do you say we write John Hopkins tomorrow and tell him to start the legal things going?"

"I'm speechless."

"Maybe he can think of something to cut down on the publicity a little. I'll ask him. It would be nice if the whole thing could be kept private."

"That's the least of our worries," I said lightly. "I'm wondering about the visit we'll be getting from a court officer to look over the house."

"Why?"

"Suppose your platoon system breaks down?"

Frank smiled. "It won't. I'm not worried . . . strangely enough, I'm not concerned at all—about anything."

This was how we finally decided on the largest adoption proceedings in California history.

XX

It was during this period that we received our first inquiry from an advertising agency named Young & Rubicam. One of their clients was the Langendorf Bread Company, a West Coast bakery, and they wanted the Beardsleys to appear in a series of television ads endorsing the bread. It was too fantastic for Frank and me to actually believe. But the representative came to visit us.

He was a very intelligent and persuasive young man, who has since become a friend, and who somehow made it seem perfectly logical that the Beardsley family would sit for TV cameras and endorse the use of a particular bread. I smothered down such questions as what possible influence our endorsement would have on other families and my general reluctance to have any further publicity, and decided to see what Frank thought when we were alone.

The young man really began to get excited when he learned the amount of bread that we used in a day. Frank enjoyed the young man's enthusiasm, but I don't think he took the possibility of our appearing on television very seriously. We didn't mention the proposal to the children at all, thinking there was no sense getting them excited about something that would probably never work out. Then, some days later, the man from the agency returned with a firm offer of a contract which would give us more money than Frank's salary for an entire year. I suppose it is always surprising when a person not in show business encounters these things and realizes the amount of money that is spent on advertisement and entertainment and has to contrast it with a lifetime of hard work and very ordinary pay. The man left the contracts so that we could have a family lawyer look at them and talk the proposal over with the children.

The children's reaction was hilarious. First they expressed disbelief. Why in the world would anyone want to put the Beardsley family on television? Then their reactions underwent a quick change, the girls wondering how they would look, the older boys mugging a little, the younger boys rather confused, but willing to go along if Michael, Rusty, and Greg said it was the thing to do.

Mike was very matter-of-fact. He said, "Dad, this will help the whole family out, and I imagine that even if they want us to do a song and dance we can get through it if we're giving the family income a boost."

Then the girls asked what they would have to do. "Would we just sit there and eat bread?"

I held my hand up. "You won't have to do anything that is embarrassing for you," I told them. "They will advise us as to

111

what typical family shots they want. They want some, naturally, with the family, probably in the kitchen, maybe during a meal, and maybe a group picture. They may also want you to sing their commercial, as a family."

Frankly, I managed to present a braver front than I actually felt toward this whole business. But, as Frank's lawyer said, it was the thing to do; and it would supplement our income. I was certainly willing to go along just as Mike was. We all were, so Frank and I signed a contract and waited for the next step.

The filming of the commercials took some twelve days. It was much more complex than I had imagined. The children were wonderful. I knew from the director and the cameramen and the men in charge of the lighting as well as from the people from the agency that they behaved as well as any professional acting group.

The first day we did have one mishap. We had the family all arranged in the living room and we were just about to start filming. I was mentally congratulating all of the children on their seeming professionalism when the director suddenly began to count heads. Two were missing: Teresa and Germaine had wandered off while the crew was preparing the lighting and getting the cameras ready. I found them in their playroom very matter-of-factly playing with their dolls.

I had an idea from reading old movie columns that a mistake in production could cost a fortune. But everybody was extremely polite about it. They even treated it as a joke. But I noticed that from then on the director always counted the children very carefully before he began filming.

So it came about that we landed in practically everyone's living room and our pictures were hurrying down the street on bread trucks. I had some doubts about the dignity of the whole thing, and yet I knew how much it would mean to these children in the future. As for the children themselves, they were quite pleased to be on television. The girls in particular acted a little as if they had broken into show business. Greg, with his usual wit, summed up the older boys' reaction when he told Frank, "Dad, it's going to be a little rough at school. I'm sure some joker is going to start calling us the *Bread*sleys."

112

XXI

Somehow it seemed that since the birth of Joseph John things had been resolving themselves for us. We found ourselves looking forward to the adoption proceedings, anxious to have an opinion rendered that would add judicial approval to something Frank and I had always known—that these children had been given a good home, and that we were more than capable of providing for them in every way. Interestingly enough, we were no longer concerned with the publicity we knew would result. And finally one day we received a notice.

The Superior Court for the State of California in Monterey County is located in Salinas. It was from this court that we received notification of an impending visit from one of the court's officers in the matter of the adoption of the North and Beardsley children. The officer, the order said, would also spend a short time talking with the children themselves.

When we told the children they were delighted. All of us are proud of our house—its comfort, cleanliness, and spaciousness. The children help to keep it nice because of this pride, and when the word goes out that a guest is to be given the grand tour (and almost without exception every guest we've had has insisted on it), each child is eager to show off his or her room. "This is mine." "Isn't it nice?" "See what a good job I do?" are the remarks the visitor is peppered with. I'm always amazed, in fact, at how (quite by accident, of course) each child seems to be at his own particular spot when the tour gets to his part of the house.

No, I knew we had nothing to fear from the court officer's visit. Our lawyer had told us it would be more or less of a formality. Still, John Hopkins had shown so much faith in us that I wanted the investigator to see a home that would in every way live up to this faith. Wouldn't any mother? Suppose, I thought, the investigator were someone who disapproved of us sight unseen? No matter what type of man he might be we all wanted him to see a home that—whatever his own personal feelings were—would make him return to the court with a report that would be unequivocal in its approval.

On the morning chosen for the officer's visit, I had everything in the house running on time. But as I was walking through the living room to check Joseph John, I heard an ominous gurgling in the downstairs toilet adjoining the older boys' study. I thought: Oh, no, the plumbing could not go wrong today. Yet there was the sound which I had come to recognize as a symptom of trouble. I suspect that although we had made changes in the house to accommodate eighteen children, including three more bathrooms, the pipe line leading from our house to the street below was too small to accommodate all the water and waste that came tumbling out of the Beardsley house. Frank, on the other hand, invariably took the attitude that someone had dropped something into one of the toilets (usually, in his judgment, a girl's hairbrush).

Having survived a number of plumbing misfortunes and having carefully watched the plumbers work, I thought I could handle the situation myself. I was glad Frank was shopping, for although in every other area he's very handy around the house, plumbing is his Waterloo. Maybe during his many long years on the ocean, living with hundreds of men on combat ships, he overlooked the requirement of a "need to know" in this area! I headed for the downstairs bathroom. Greg was already there, looking a bit puzzled about the water which was now bubbling up from the drain in the shower.

I said urgently, "Greg, make certain no one uses any water. Get a wrench to take off the joint under the sink and haul up an outside hose and bring it in here . . ."

Greg looked almost sad. "Which should I do first?"

"All of them, right now," I said, in a tone his father might have used. He started up the stairs on the double. I took a plunger and started working furiously on the shower drain.

Greg returned with Nicky and Tommy, sending them out to hook up the garden hose. He had the wrench and began to take off the joint beneath the sink. There was method in my madness. Some plumbers merely used the plunger. Others hooked up a hose, flushed water down the sink drain and cleared the obstruction. Others used the same technique on an outside drain. Now I intended to test all three methods before calling anyone. Greg removed the joint, I worked the plunger faster while the water mounted dangerously close to the sill of the shower. Tommy brought in the green garden hose and in with him marched Phillip in his baseball cap, Germaine, and Gerry, followed by Cindy, the dog.

"Out of the house!"

They looked at the hose, the rising water, Greg by the open drain, the wild woman with plunger in hand, and disappeared.

Now Greg took the hose from Tommy. "Stay there by the door," he told Tommy, "and when I tell you, you yell to Nicky to turn the hose on." In the next few minutes my plan went into action. We tried all the plumbers' tricks I had seen. We flushed the toilet, turned the hose on full into the sink drain, and I plunged like mad in the shower. The result was that the toilet, the sink drain, and the shower all overflowed at once. And then I called the plumber.

Because of previous experiences, Frank had carefully instructed the children never to delay the plumber "in the rounds of his duty." Long conversations with plumbers cost serious money. So when the doorbell rang Phillip was immediately at the kitchen door announcing, "The plumber man is here."

Unfortunately, when the "plumber man" was led to me, it was immediately apparent that he was the probation officer from the court checking our adoption procedure. Without batting an eye, he withdrew gracefully when I asked Phillip to take him to the living room, where I joined him after a quick change.

He assured me his visit was only a formality and I sat and answered questions about our income, our expenses, plans for the children; questions about their education. I wondered how Greg was doing downstairs and hoped no one would run any water anywhere in the house.

Fortunately, the rest of the house was running smoothly. The older boys, Mike and Rusty, were on the ladders cleaning the outside windows, which had been badly spotted by one of our infrequent winter rainstorms. Everyone was busy at his charge. Discounting one disheveled mother, we could not have staged a more impressive setting.

The gentleman looked around at the girls in the kitchen. Rosemary, Janette, and Colleen were all busy preparing the lunch, making peanut butter and jelly sandwiches. Louise was at her very favorite occupation, which was taking care of Joseph John in the living room. The visitor was very official, very proper and reserved. At first I thought it must be that he had written out so many adverse reports that he was prepared for the worst. But then I realized that it was really because he felt that he was intruding.

We went through the questions of income, and this was rather our weak point, I felt, for Frank's salary, as most service salaries are, was low, and the Social Security that I received was minimal.

Then I guided him through the house, showing him how the children had been arranged by age and disposition, showing him their charges, and going over all the logistics that Frank had figured out to make this house work. Perhaps because he was a trained professional, the officer was mostly noncommittal to what he saw. Since most visitors who saw the house and the way everything had been arranged and worked out were enthusiastic, his lack of comment threw me for a few minutes. Soon I realized, however, that he was only doing his job, and that in reality he was trying to be as friendly, warm, and interested as his work would permit. But friendly or not, I was determined not to bring him downstairs again, where Greg was still bailing water from the flooded shower.

At the end of his visit, the officer asked to talk to the children. Those who were over twelve had some papers to sign, and this part they really enjoyed. They went through the full range of their repertoire of humor before putting down their signature. "What's it worth to you if I sign?" or "Shall I be formal now, Mrs. Beardsley, and call you Mother, or can I still call you Mom?"

Except for the flood on the lower floor, I felt that the visit from the court officer had gone well. I couldn't know whether or not the spirit of our home interested him, or if he had noted how happy the children were. But in trying to look at our home through his objective eyes I realized that at the very least he would see that we had a good physical environment for the children. When he left he seemed almost apologetic for having had to visit us at all.

Frank came home a while later with the station wagon full of groceries.

"Everything O.K.?"

"Fine. The plumbing went wrong."

"Someone dropped a hairbrush down one of the toilets, no doubt."

116

"I don't know what caused the trouble."

"Don't worry—for fifty dollars the plumber'll tell us."

Phillip came in wearing his baseball cap, followed by Teresa and Joan. Cindy sat down outside with a grunt.

"The probation officer from the court came by," I said nonchalantly.

Frank perked up. "How did it go?"

"Very smoothly. I was surprised."

"Well, John said it would only be a formality."

Phillip said, "Daddy?"

"Yes."

"You know what I've decided to become?"

"No, Phillip."

"A plumber."

"Wonderful, Phillip. You'll save the Beardsleys a fortune."

XXII

Another winter deepened, and in the slow process of the law we heard nothing from the court. Frank and I felt confident that the adoption would go smoothly, but found ourselves impatient over its delay. The children kept asking us when it would happen, for we had planned that the day of the adoption would be a festive one. Even John Hopkins and his lovely wife Lorraine had promised to join us that day for a party.

There were times, during the waiting, that I found myself thinking of the coming proceedings with annoyance that our society's legal rules were so constructed as to make this name change necessary. The feelings of good people had been hurt as a result. But such thoughts didn't linger for long, for immediately I'd remember how much this meant to our children. Their welfare had to be our greatest concern. And so we waited for the complicated machinery of the law to send us our happy summons, until after a while we got so used to waiting and became so busy with other things that we almost developed an easy patience about it.

Finally a letter arrived from John Hopkins telling us where to appear. John, bless his heart, added that the judge had agreed to hear our case on a Saturday so that we might avoid the publicity such an adoption would involve. If he held court then, the proceedings would not have to be listed on the docket. Few of the curious would be about, and the public would not be admitted. It would be as private as a public hearing could be. I remember thinking that Mr. Hopkins was not only a fine lawyer but a man very sensitive to such American tribal customs as publicity.

We were to bring all the children involved to the court and, of course, ourselves, so that the court could make a "judgment of adoption." The mere legal phraseology of the papers was a bit awesome.

Salinas is a city on a plain, surrounded by mountains. It is a celery and lettuce center, and is bordered by farms and newly located industry. We arrived there in two cars, all of us in our Sunday best, and drove into a parking area across the street from the courthouse. It was a relatively new building, impressive, built in the California style.

Our final destination within the building, the Superior Court, was like a stage setting. It was new and quite modern, and deserted as it was now, I found myself taking note of its details. The windows were not institutional in any way; they each had four panes. I noticed all these things, I suppose, to keep from being nervous as we sat there -Frank and I and our nineteen children—and waited for a judge named Anthony Brazil to pronounce that all these children who as far as we were concerned already belonged to us in every way, did so in legal fact. When our own case was announced, however, the room itself became unimportant and I was conscious only of the court clerk's formal tones.

"In the matter of the adoption of Colleen Marie North, Janette Deen North, Nicholas Richard North Thomas Roderick North, Jean Louise North Phillip Anthony North, Gerald Joseph North, and Teresa Rose North, minors in a question for a judgment of adoption . . ."

The clerk paused, and the judge leaned forward. ". . . Will the petitioner, Francis Louis Beardsley, please step forward."

Frank stepped from the benches behind the railing to the area in front of the counsels' table.

Frank was very solemn. Square-shouldered, square-jawed,

118

in a blue suit, a white shirt, and a blue tie, his shoes shining, hair brushed back, he was the image of a relaxed man. But then, of course, I'm biased.

The judge looked at him for a moment and then said, "Would the minors please step forward."

I had no way of knowing what the judge thought or what was in the reports which he was reading as he asked the minors to step forward and each of the Norths filed out of the spectators' seats as they might file out of a pew in church and stood beside Frank before the judge.

The judge asked Frank, "You are married to the mother of these children?"

"On September 9, 1961."

"You are an adult and you are ten years older than each and all of these minor children?"

Frank said this was true.

The judge went on. "Has your wife, as consent is required by law, consented to the adoption of the minor children by you, and filed this consent with the Clerk of the Court? And have you been examined by a probation officer of this county?"

Frank said, "Yes, and I have."

The judge looked down and said, "Would Colleen Marie North please step forward."

Colleen did.

The judge said, "You're over the age of twelve. Do you consent to this adoption in a manner prescribed by law?"

Colleen smiled her very beautiful smile and said, "Yes, sir, I do."

The judge turned again to Frank.

"Will you, therefore, execute an agreement in the presence of the court that the children shall be treated in all respects as your lawful children? And will you also present an affidavit that the children are proper subjects for adoption, that your home is suitable for the children, and that the interests of the children will be promoted by their adoption by you?"

Frank said that he would execute such an agreement.

The judge went through some papers before him and studied them for some time. These must have been the report of the court officer who had visited our home. Then he looked down at the children for a moment and again looked at Frank. When he spoke this time his words reflected his own personal feelings.

119

"I am happy to be here today," he said, "happy to be here on what is such a great and wonderful day for all of you. So often this courtroom is the scene of unhappy struggle and sadness. So seldom is there a welcome and pleasant change from it. I want you to know, therefore, that this adoption—as have been other adoptions over which I have presided—is one of those occasions . . ." There was a momentary silence in the courtroom. Then Judge Brazil cleared his throat and resumed reading from the papers before him.

"It is ordered that the hereinbefore-named minors, and each of them, be adopted by petitioner, and these persons shall hereafter sustain towards each other all legal obligations of parent and children, and shall have all rights and be under all the duties of such a relationship, including all legal duties of custody and support and inheritance. It is further ordered that the children shall hereafter bear the family name of the petitioner and shall be known as Colleen Marie Beardsley, Janette Deen Beardsley, Nicholas Richard Beardsley, Thomas Roderick Beardsley, Jean Louise Beardsley, Phillip Anthony Beardsley, Gerald Joseph Beardsley, and Teresa Rose Beardsley."

There was a brief pause. And then the judge went through the same formality with me, much more quickly this time. He concluded with the same order.

In the quiet that followed, the children slowly broke out in smiles as they recognized they were all one family. Had we not been in a courtroom I'm sure they'd have raised a big cheer. Instead, as if to match the dignity of the court, they went toward each other, each toward his favorite brother or sister, and embraced, or held hands, or just continued to smile.

Frank and I were quite overcome and held onto each other, and little Joseph John seemed to become the center of everybody's attention. The judge had now completely forgotten his judicial manner and looked down and said, "Is that little Joseph John? Well, he's one little fellow that won't have to be adopted."

And if the children had burst forth with a rousing cheer then I don't think anyone would have frowned. It would have expressed all the wonder and joy that was inside of us. For this whole procedure meant that the merger of these two families had worked; that the love between Frank and me had been blessed; that the hand of God was on our shoulders and the love of God was in our hearts; and that we could face anything we had to face in the future, knowing that we had only to ask for the strength to bear the burden and it would all be given. You had only to ask and you received.

Postscript

Some time after the adoption, and most markedly after the birth of our second child, Helen Monica, on April 19, 1964, I noticed that people seemed finally to have accepted the idea of the Beardsleys. It was almost as if the world had nodded its head and decided to go along with us—as if people who had formerly looked upon us as a strange novelty accepted the adoption and the birth of Helen Monica as a sign that we were indeed a family like every other. Frank and I had always done what we thought was right. We fell in love and married. In doing so we were able to provide parents for eighteen lovely children. We feel, therefore, that ours is a true love story. We hope that it will never have an ending.

If the world is going along with us, I think we have decided to go along with the world a bit, too. We still don't understand our national celebrity but its effects no longer bother us. We barely take note any more of the sightseeing bus that daily stops across the street while its occupants gaze at our house. Such things we take in our stride now and accept as a charming public eccentricity.

The number of years that a family remains together are limited. For our family, because of the comparatively short time we have all been together, these few years have been looked on as golden ones, too quickly passed.

Already Mike, for so long the children's idol, and Rusty, for so long their dearest advisor, have chosen to serve their tour of duty in the Marines before college. Now Greg, with his quick humor and smile, is the oldest at home. The little ones are growing up. The atmosphere of the house keeps changing. A mood and time so precious to us is lost, while at the same time our memories and hearts are enriched. And for Frank and myself, our experience has the mystery and grace of love—the love of God, the love of family, the love of two people for each other.